Confessions of a CPA

Confessions of a CPA

Why What I Was Taught To Be True Has Turned Out Not To Be

Bryan S. Bloom

Bryan S. Bloom

CONTENTS ▌

Dedication

To my extraordinary wife, Pamela, from whom I receive love, support, and inspiration to pursue the important things in life. And to my children, Callie and Corrie, who remind me daily of the value of making investments in the generations ahead.

BRYAN S. BLOOM

Foreword

I joined the financial services industry in 2003. My purpose was, and still is, to positively impact people's lives so they nor their family would ever have to worry about money, or where it comes from, ever again. After a short time of being in this profession, I noticed a few things.

Money is a sensitive subject. Often, it is more sensitive than even politics, race, or religion.

Most people have been socially programmed to believe a certain way when it comes to how money works.

The average person has no idea of how true wealth building works and worse they have been taught that transferring money to large financial institutions and giving up control of their money is the only way to build true wealth.

Over time, I learned more and more about people's beliefs and the history of our profession. My experience taught me that these beliefs have been ingrained in generation after generation. How people felt about money has been going on for decades!

Since as far back as The Great Depression Era, people have been taught, by a variety of financial institutions, the same traditional methods of how to accumulate wealth, buy a home, save for retirement, pay off debt, save for college, invest, and pay their taxes. While all those topics are meaningful, there is one big problem with all of them; the traditional methods don't work!! If they did, everyone who listened to them would be rich, but they're not.

The United States is among the wealthiest countries to ever exist on planet Earth. Yet, nearly 50% of Americans do not make more than $50,000 per year and around 12% of our citizens are in poverty. Why?

Prior to getting into this profession, I was among the large population of Americans who did not know much about money or how it worked either. I knew how to pay bills and write checks, but I did not know how to invest and grow money without giving up control of what little money I had to a financial institution. It was only after being "reactive" to my mistakes that I realized the traditional methods of financial planning was "losing" me money unknowingly and unnecessarily. As it turns out, I was taught the same things everyone else is taught.

It wasn't until later in my career, when I met Bryan, that I began to truly understand the rules of money and how the "system" works. Bryan helped me see the world of money through a different kind of lens. He helped me learn what he knew to be true about how growing money works. Among other things, his take on the "miracle" of compound interest has changed my life for the better. When I began to see things differently and implement his strategies, I noticed the difference between my assets and liabilities widen. One of the great things about Bryan's strategy is that I was able to implement it without giving up control of my money to someone else OR decreasing my current standard of living and pinning myself to a budget. The money I used to improve my financial situation was already "in play". Bryan showed me how to use it more efficiently.

Bryan has dedicated his professional life to learning everything about how money truly works. His CPA background makes him well-rounded for this type of profession. His understanding of a complicated subject matter and ability to explain things to people so they understand it makes him a great teacher. You don't need a CPA designation, a finance degree, or years of experience as a financial advisor to build wealth for yourself. You just need to follow the ideas in this book. They are unlike anything you have ever heard before, with the added benefit of.... they actually work!

In Bryan's mind, if there was a way, he could teach you everything he has learned over his entire career in the time it takes you to read this book, then your financial situation can change for the better as well. Bryan's knowledge, experience and insight are impeccable. Confessions of a CPA is a must read for anyone who wonders why things they thought were true about money turn out not to be true. "Why am I doing everything I'm told to do, but do not seem to be any further ahead?" "Why didn't anyone tell me that?" "Why do I not have any more money, even though I'm saving like I should be?" Bryan's ability to break down one of the most sensitive and complicated subjects in our society, money, is amazing! He will give you his ideas and thoughts about how to build true wealth. He will show you where the information is and help you realize it's always been there, but no one has taught you to find it. He will give you the secrets of how to build wealth and keep control of your money along the way. He will teach you what the Banks, IRS, and the big Wall Street firms have known for decades about how to build massive wealth! These techniques are the keys to building true wealth. You will be able to build wealth for you and your family, not for the families of people who work for the large financial institutions in the United States.

Enjoy!

Jeff Seeburger
President
The America Group Financial Services Company, Inc.

Have an impactful day.

BRYAN S. BLOOM

Acknowledgements

There are so many people who have influenced my career and encouraged me to write this book, all of whom have made this book possible.

First and foremost, I am grateful to my Heavenly Father, the Yahweh of the Old Testament of the Bible who lets me call him "Abba Father," and His Son, Jesus Christ, who is my personal Lord and Savior.

I would also like to than my wife, Pam, and my children, Callie Sederquist and Corrie Musgrave, for their love an encouragement to write and create.

My extended family has been influential as well: my parents, John and Jackie Bloom, and Pam's parents, Harold and Annie Jean Ray. Thank you. My first client was my brother Jeff. Thank you for letting me experiment on you.

I would be remiss if I did not mention my colleagues at The America Group and my close friends in the financial services profession. Each one of them has helped me refine my thinking about what I was taught to be true. Each time I realized another fallacy of traditional financial thinking these guys verified my thinking. Relationships ebb and flow and some are more influential than others at different junctures of a career. Those who have influenced me, you know who you are and my gratitude overflows for you and your influence at just the right time.

I will always be grateful for to the dedicated individuals at all levels at Ohio National Financial Services. Your acknowledgement of me with two of the highest honors is truly humbling. The Tschanz Lifetime Achievement Award recognized my achievements over my entire lifetime, not just my tenure at Ohio National. The Chairman's Navigator Award recognized "the highest standard of professionalism dedication, commitment and leadership". I received the award during the 100th anniversary of Ohio National Financial Services; presented only for the second time. It is given to an individual "who is of exceptional character and integrity. I am the only person to have been presented with both awards. Thank you for your confidence in me by granting me with these honors.

Common Sense

The simple definition of common sense is good sense and sound judgement in practical matters. It is the basic ability to perceive, understand, judge, and apply that which is shared by most people. It is the knack for seeing things as they are and doing things as they ought to be done. When something in your gut is telling you what to do next, that may be common sense guiding you. It is the urge to trust your instincts and listen to your intuition.

In this edition of Confessions of a CPA, I have included quotes accumulated throughout the years from people regarding their understanding of common sense. I have included these quotes because the most common comment I received from the first edition was, "that just makes so much common sense".

Some quotes are whimsical and witty, while others are serious and philosophical. Some are from the 21st century and others are from long ago. The inspiration for including quotes regarding common sense came from Thomas Paine, whose work Common Sense, laid a foundation for the American Colonies to resist Great Britain and fight for independence. Sometimes merely asking common sense questions provides unique clarity to understand complex situations.

1

The Miracle of Compound Interest

"Common sense is the collection of prejudices acquired by age eighteen."
Albert Einstein

"Common sense is seeing things as they are;
and doing things as they ought to be."
Harriet Beecher Stowe

"Those who understand interest, earn it.
Those who don't, pay it."
Albert Einstein

Albert Einstein said, "the miracle of compound interest is the eighth wonder of the world." Whether you are looking at the seven wonders of the ancient world, the seven wonders of the natural world, or the seven wonders of the modern world, many would agree and add the miracle of compound interest as the eighth wonder. It has risen to such heights because of the exponential curve it creates rises to heights that command our attention. It does not matter whether you save a single sum or a series of amounts; when left alone to grow, it grows exponentially. Then, not only do your deposits earn interest, but the interest your deposits earned, earns interest as well. The potential is unlimited.

It does not matter whether you are saving for a child's education, your retirement years, or even to leave a financial legacy from your physical lifetime; the miracle occurs. Let us consider the first two of these, since these are two lifetime events most people plan for. Proper attention to these two, will help you achieve the third as a by-product of your planning.

Suppose you have a child today and wanted to begin their college savings fund immediately. To have a sufficient sum of money available to pay for four years of public university education 18 years from now (Source: Trends in College Pricing, 2019. The College Board), you would need to begin saving $9,000 each year. If you did that, you would save $162,000 of your own money, but your account would have grown to $265,000 if you were able to earn 5% on that money for each of the 18 years. The extra $100,000 comes from not only your money earning interest, but also from your interest earning interest. That would be enough to pay over $65,000 per year for four years of your child's education. Yes, that is a lot, but it is merely today's cost of tuition, fees, and related living expenses, inflated by 6%.

At the end of the four years of education, the university now has the $265,000, and you have zero. Not only does the university have the money, but it can also earn interest on the money, which was once your opportunity. In essence you have not only paid for the college education but have also transferred your potential miracle to the University. Now it has become their miracle!

If you wanted to accumulate the magic retirement amount of $1,000,000 between your college graduation and age 65— a mere 43 years—you would need to save less per year than you need for Junior's education. In fact, at an earnings rate of 5%, you would need to save $6,660 per year. Why less? Because the retirement miracle has 43 years to run, not just 18.

Let us combine these two ideas to further understand this miracle. If the college funding of $9,000 per year were to run for eighteen years and then that value continued to earn for another 47 years, instead of transferring the miracle to the university, your son or daughter would have $2,633,512 to retire with. Let us take it one last step. What if your son or daughter added their own $6,660 to your college savings for them? They could retire on over $3.8 million! Now do you see why it is called a miracle? It also begs the question, just how valuable is that college degree?

Some financial advisers would lead you to believe that you can earn more than 5%; indeed, you might, and if you do, the miracle gets even better. If you can add just 1% to this last example, at age 65 you would have almost $5.8 million. Many advisers still believe you can earn 8% in the market over the long run, which would yield a miraculous result of $13 million. And if you listen to popular financial talk radio, they will tell you that you can earn 12%. If the miracle grew at the rate of 12%, which might be even more miraculous than compound interest itself, you would have $67 million!

If the miracle of compound interest is true, why aren't we all rich by now? Even if you earned 8% on a $100-per-month savings plan over your working career, you would have $450,000 at age sixty-five. Are you on target? If what you were taught to be true turned out not to be, when would you want to know? Keep reading.

Look at the following graph. This is $9,000 per year being saved for 18 years at 5%. Notice that the graph does not look exponential.

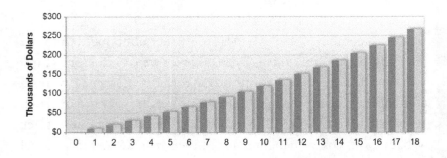

But look at the university's graph after the money is transferred to them. Notice the linear nature of the first 18 years, and the exponential growth after the money is in the hands of the university. I am assuming the same 5% rate of return.

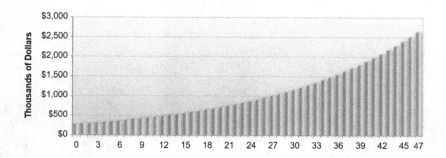

This graph assumes that the $265,000 paid to the University is held by the University until your age 65 (4 years of college and 43 years after college). This represents the cost to your retirement: $2,633,512.

Lesson #1: What I was taught to be true about the miracle of compound interest that has turned out not to be true, is because there is no allowance for spending money during the compounding period. When we spend the miracle and transfer it to someone else, the compounding stops for us.

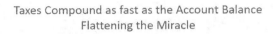

Taxes Compound as fast as the Account Balance
Flattening the Miracle

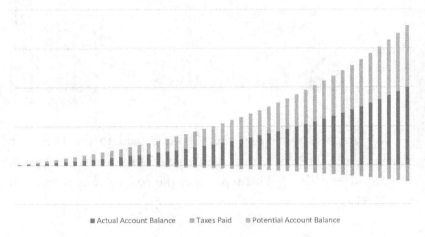

■ Actual Account Balance   ▦ Taxes Paid   ▦ Potential Account Balance

This lesson is compounded due to taxes. Even if we do not choose to spend the miracle, we may be forced to spend some of it to pay the taxes due on the annual growth of the account. If we do not pay it from the account, we must compromise our lifestyle to pay the income taxes from our budget. Funds to pay income taxes due on the growth must come from somewhere, either from the account itself or from our discretionary spending budget. If the money comes from the account, the miracle cannot work, and if it comes from a compromised lifestyle, that does not sound like much fun either.

Let us go back to the million-dollar retirement. Because Uncle Sam demands that you pay taxes on the interest and dividends you earn, as you earn them, the million-dollar potential is stunted greatly. Paying a combined federal and state tax rate of 30% on the earnings, as earned, reduces your miracle to $667,000.

If you add the tax on just the growth each year, the tax you pay is $163,000. However, the miracle of compound interest is now working against you. Because the taxes due were extracted from the account, they were no longer in the account to earn the compounding interest. A dollar spent is no longer available to ever earn again; that is called opportunity cost. The opportunity cost of paying the taxes out of the account is another $170,000. The opportunity cost is more than the actual interest cost! Add the two together, subtract the total from the original million you thought you would have, and you end up with $667,000. Not exactly the million-dollar retirement you had in mind.

As fast as the exponential curve is increasing, while interest is compounding, the taxes due and the lost opportunity from paying the tax are increasing at the same rate. The taxes due and the lost opportunity from paying the tax are eroding your compounding.

Look at the actual account bar; it is nearly linear again. The taxes stole your miracle.

The graph may seem out of proportion. Why isn't the gap between the potential account balance equal to the taxes paid? Because the potential account balance reflects not only the taxes paid but also what those taxes paid could have earned had you not paid them.

Lesson #2: What I was taught to be true about the miracle of compound interest that has turned out not to be true, is that because of the taxes due on the growth, the miracle will be tarnished by reducing the amount of money you would otherwise expect.

There is at least one more reason why what I was taught to be true about compound interest that has not turned out to be true. When we realize it does not work, we quit.

Let us use the example of someone who wants to invest $5,000 per year and experiences a 9% rate of return on their investments. Slowly, the account gains momentum, but by the time the exponential curve begins to show itself in year eighteen, you realize the annual tax due eventually exceeds your investment in the account:

Year	Annual Deposit	Beginning Balance	Annual Interest	Annual Tax Due
1	5,000	5,000	450	(135)
2	5,000	10,450	941	(282)
3	5,000	16,391	1,475	(443)
4	5,000	22,866	2,058	(617)
5	5,000	29,924	2,693	(808)
6	5,000	37,617	3,386	(1,016)
7	5,000	46,002	4,140	(1,242)
8	5,000	55,142	4,963	(1,489)
9	5,000	65,105	5,859	(1,758)
10	5,000	75,965	6,837	(2,051)
11	5,000	87,801	7,902	(2,371)
12	5,000	100,704	9,063	(2,719)
13	5,000	114,767	10,329	(3,099)
14	5,000	130,096	11,709	(3,513)
15	5,000	146,805	13,212	(3,964)
16	5,000	165,017	14,852	(4,455)
17	5,000	184,869	16,638	(4,991)
18	5,000	206,507	18,586	(5,576)
End of Year 18 Balance		225,093		
Total Tax Paid				40,529

You get to year eighteen, and you realize that you are paying more in taxes annually than you are adding to the account annually. Why keep saving when all you are doing is creating a tax bill equal to the annual savings? That is an incredibly good question, and you stop saving!

For those inclined to stop saving, the thinking goes like this. In the early years, it is not so bad. In year one, you are paying only an extra $135 in taxes. You hardly notice it, and perhaps it only reduces your tax refund at the end of the year. In year two, the taxes are only $147 more than in year one, but again you do not notice. It is like the heat being turned up slowly; the cold-water warms, it grows in temperature, eventually it gets hot, and before you know it, your goose is cooked, and what you are saving is being spent on taxes! As the chart shows, your account is worth over $200,000, but it has started to cost you more in taxes than what you are depositing each year.

Lesson #3: What I was taught to be true about the miracle of compound interest that has turned out not to be true, is that when we realize the impact of having to pay taxes on the growth of our account, we may stop saving or investing.

Now consider where the tax dollars are coming from each year. They are not from your investments because you know that would stunt the growth. The taxes are coming from one less vacation dinner for your family in year one ($135); one less day of vacation by year three ($443); right sizing your cruise vacation from a balcony suite to an inner cabin by year ten ($2,051); to eliminating your family vacation all together by year 18 ($5,576). This represents just one choice regarding how you might change your lifestyle to save and invest, when you misunderstand the miracle of compounding interest and the silent enemy: the miracle of compounding taxes. The point is that for every tax dollar paid out of pocket, that is one less lifestyle dollar you have available to spend the next year. What will you choose to eliminate from your lifestyle?

Perhaps the answer is to net the taxes due from the investment, so your lifestyle is not compromised. The impact of that may be surprising. Here is the same chart, reducing the investment each year by the taxes due:

Year	Annual Deposit	Begging Balance	Annual Interest	Annual Tax Due
1	5,000	5,000	450	(135)
2	5,000	10,315	928	(279)
3	5,000	15,965	1,437	(431)
4	5,000	21,971	1,977	(593)
5	5,000	28,355	2,552	(766)
6	5,000	35,141	3,163	(949)
7	5,000	42,355	3,812	(1,144)
8	5,000	50,023	4,502	(1,351)
9	5,000	58,175	5,236	(1,571)
10	5,000	66,840	6,016	(1,805)
11	5,000	76,051	6,845	(2,053)
12	5,000	85,842	7,226	(2,318)
13	5,000	96,250	8,663	(2,599)
14	5,000	107,314	9,658	(2,987)
15	5,000	119,075	10,717	(3,215)
16	5,000	131,576	11,842	(3,553)
17	5,000	144,866	13,038	(3,911)
18	5,000	158,992	14,309	(4,293)
End of Year 18 Balance		169,009		
Total Tax Paid				33,861

You may want to flip back and forth to appreciate the difference between paying your taxes from your lifestyle and netting your taxes out of your investment. At first glance, it appears we may have found an answer. The actual taxes paid by netting the tax from your account is less by $6,687. That is good, right? Not necessarily. Just because you pay less tax, does not mean you have more money. Look at the end of year 18 balance. You may have paid $6,687 less in taxes, but you have $56,084 less money! You pay less income tax because you have less money.

Lesson #4: What I was taught to be true about the miracle of compound interest that has turned out not to be true, is that when you net anything from your account, you have less money invested, therefore you end up with less money at the end.

What else do you pay for from your investment account? Emergencies you haven't budgeted for? Purchases you planned to save for before you spend, like a new car, a college education, a wedding...? Investment fees?

Lesson #5: What I was taught to be true about the miracle of compound interest that has turned out not to be true, is that Einstein was wrong, it is not the 8th wonder of the world. There is nothing miraculous about compound interest. The only way it works, is if you do not spend your money. The only way Einstein can be right is if his 8th wonder of the world included the word "uninterrupted". The miracle of uninterrupted compound interest.

2

Taxes

"Common sense told us that when you put a big tax on something, the people will produce less of it.
So, we cut the people's tax rates, and the people produced more
than ever before."
Ronald Reagan

"There are two systems of taxation in this country...
one for the informed and one for the uninformed."
Judge Learned Hand

"Tax reform is taking the taxes off things that have been taxed in
the past
and putting taxes on things that haven't been taxed before."
Art Buchwald

Compound interest is the most important foundational principle to understand. Taxation is the second.

The most important discipline you should develop is learning how to prepare your own income tax return. It is only in struggling through this task that you can begin to understand what is going on. There is nothing wrong in paying a professional tax preparer to prepare your return, but you should do so only after you have done them yourself. Think of a professional tax preparer as the teacher who grades your exam.

Income taxation dates to the civil war when it was determined that tariffs and excise taxes were not enough to both run a government and finance the war effort. So, the United States of America assessed an income tax on anyone who earned more than $600. The Confederate States of America assessed a similar tax but only on those who earned over $1,000. Income taxation was abolished in 1872.

A significant event in the history of the U. S. came in 1895, when the U. S. Supreme Court ruled that the income tax that was established in 1864 was unconstitutional.

That lasted until 1913, when the Internal Revenue Code was established with a single paragraph as the 16th Amendment of the U. S. Constitution. "The Congress shall have power to lay and collect taxes on incomes, from whatever source derived, without apportionment among the several States, and without regard to any census or enumeration." Today, the Internal Revenue Code is anywhere from 4,000 to 1.3 million pages long depending on the source. The scariest citation I found regarding the length of the Code came from The

Taxpayer Advocate service of Congress, who told Congress in 2008, "The Code has grown so long that it has become challenging even to figure out how long it is." No wonder you are afraid to do it yourself!

The enactment of "The Current Tax Payment Act" in 1943, began the process of the federal government hiding from the American public just how much we pay in income taxes. It was sold as an emergency wartime necessity, but just as with so many other things, what is first an emergency eventually becomes a necessity. Withholding income taxes from a wage earners paycheck effectively hides the amount of taxes we pay from our consciousness. Ask someone how much they are paid, and they will tell you their take home pay, not their actual wage. This is regrettable, because if the people who pay taxes realized how much the government was taking from them, they would be infuriated.

Over the years, I have talked with numerous individuals about their income taxes. The most disheartening response I get to the question, "How much do you pay in taxes?", is the response, "I don't pay taxes, I get a refund." This has become the status quo in the United States. Ronald Reagan once said, "Status quo is Latin for, the mess we are in."

This is the first misperception about taxes. If you get a tax refund at the end of the year, you do not pay income taxes.

Fortunately, most of what I was taught to be true about taxes has actually turned out to be true, so I want to discuss some of the misperceptions.

The second misperception regards the structure of tax rates. The U.S. income tax code uses graduated tax rates not a cliff rate. Under the graduated system of taxation, those with less income pay less per dollar earned, than those who earn more. Cliff rates would have you determine your taxable income, then find the applicable tax rate for that level of income and apply that rate to every dollar of income. Cliff rates are generally found in our system of sales tax, where everyone pays the same rate of sales tax no matter how much money they spend.

The difference is startling. The following example illustrates this point, but also indicates the level of misunderstanding among American taxpayers.

I recently worked with a couple who was preparing for retirement. In preparation they were considering paying all the taxes they had not paid while they were working (more on that in the Qualified Plan chapter) before they retired. They had not paid taxes on over $116,000. According to cliff taxation, that $116,000 would have been added to their regular income for the year and would have resulted in all their income being in the 32% tax bracket. According to their calculation, this would have resulted in total taxes paid for the year of $113,000! By not understanding the difference between cliff taxation and our current graduated system of taxation, their conclusion was that their entire nest egg might be confiscated. It is bad, but not that bad; yet.

The graduated tax rate system we use today would have resulted in a total tax bill of $67,000. Of this, $39,000 is ascribed to their regular earned income for this year. The tax on the $116,000 extra income is only $28,000. Still a lot of money, but that was their choice many years ago when they decided that they did not want to pay their taxes when due, but to defer them to the future.

Graduated rates ascribe a certain tax rate to a defined band of income. Today, the first band of $24,000 of income for a married couple is taxed at 0%. The second band covers income from $24,000 up to $43,900 and is taxed at 10%. The third band covers income from $43,900 up to $105,050 and is taxed at 12%. That means that only $62,150 is taxed at 12%, not $105,050. Currently, there are only 8 bands of income that are taxed. Of course, the last one, the 37% band is unlimited. At the height of World War II, President Franklin Roosevelt proposed 24 bands, the last one also unlimited at a tax rate of 100%. Congress talked him down to reducing the top rate to 94%.

Sometimes, we think of our average income tax rate. This is a rate not found anywhere, because it merely calculates a rate that blends all the graduated rates for an individual taxpayer's circumstance. In the example of the couple, I had just had the conversation with, without the inclusion of income that had been deferred, their average rate was 16.5% and with the inclusion of the income from which taxes had never been paid, the average rate was 19%. As your income increases so does the average tax rate you pay.

This client uncovered an untaught principle of taxation, at least one I was never taught, which leads to the third misperception. My realization of this principle only came from calculating hundreds of tax returns for people. The principle is that extraordinary income floats normal earned income into higher tax brackets. The reason this goes untaught is because the converse is taught, and it is short sided. What is taught is that extraordinary income is added on top of your ordinary income and taxed at your highest marginal tax rate.

Just the opposite is true and has dramatic implications that effects more than just your ordinary income taxes.

Lesson #1: What I was taught to be true about taxation that has turned out not to be true, is that extraordinary income is taxed first, not last, moving all other income and income tax calculations into the higher brackets.

In this example, with a joint wage income of $237,000, that would have tapped out in the 24% band of income. But, because they added $116,000 of extraordinary, non-recurring income, that is considered first in the graduated scheme of taxation we have. That extraordinary income floated some of their ordinary into the 32% bracket. You may ask, doesn't it work out to the same amount of tax paid, because of the graduated tax principles? Yes, it does, but the trickle-down effect can be enormous. It is the trickle-down effects that have caught us sleeping.

Since we have been talking about extraordinary income, what exactly is extraordinary income? I consider any unearned income as extraordinary. The U.S. tax code only requires that you pay income tax once on the money we earn. Every other income tax is dependent upon what we do with in the income we earn. Therefore, any cash flow defined as "income" over and above what we earn is extraordinary, because it did not have to be taxable in the first place. We voluntarily chose it to be taxed.

Consider the income effect on the taxation of social security. Even "tax free" income works like a float on the taxes we pay, in this example the tax we pay is on social security.

Now you may be screaming, "wait", "stop" or "time out!". "My social security is taxable when I receive it? Didn't I pay taxes on what I paid into social security all those years?" Yes, you did! "That sounds like double taxation" you exclaim. Again, you are right because it is. Our nation was established because we protested the British taxation of our tea without having any say in the tax. We call that, "Taxation without representation." It only took a bit more than 200 years to completely flip the script. The taxation of Social Security, started in 1984, was enacted into law by our Congressional process. That means that all our Senators, Representatives and President, know about this additional tax. That would be "Double taxation with representation".

We have been duped by our own investment experience into thinking that what we pay into social security is an investment in our retirement. It is not. It is insurance in case we live too long. It is social assistance. It is welfare. When you do not "need it", it is confiscated in the form of additional income taxes. In 1935, when the Social Security Act was signed into law, the average life expectancy for men was 60, and for women, 64. The earliest you could claim your "old age" insurance benefit was 65. A brilliant program! However, the first person to receive a monthly social security check nearly broke the bank. Ida May Fuller collected social security until her death at age 100. She received $22,888 in benefits. She paid $24.75 into Social Security during her three years of employment.

Social Security is really a welfare benefit paid for by an insurance premium. FICA withholding from our compensation is merely the purchase of insurance with after tax income. Just as you would purchase any insurance product, however, this is purchased through a payroll deduction. Because it is welfare, the grantor of the welfare can determine who qualifies for the financial assistance, and if you qualify for the financial assistance, how much of it you can keep. If your Social Security is less than $24,000, and that is all the extraordinary income you have, your Social Security is tax free. But your social security extraordinary income floats up into the taxable category when you include other extraordinary income from such sources as your 401(k), dividends or even tax-free municipal bond interest.

Just to be clear, if you are at normal retirement age or older and still working, the taxes due on your normal compensation is determined by layering under your compensation. First your 401(k) distribution, then your taxable social security welfare benefits. With these two sources of extraordinary income considered first, only then can you determine in what tax band your normal compensation is taxed at.

If you are married, and your $24,000 Social Security benefit is enhanced by $20,001 of either taxable, tax free (municipal bond interest) or capital gain income (dividends), part of your social security will become taxable and push your other ordinary income up to higher bands. Can you see the impact of extraordinary income tax float?

The same impact is felt when you have capital gain income from either the sale of a security or a dividend. However, capital gain extraordinary income is a double-edged sword. Not only does it float your other income into higher income bands, but it is also used on the other end as well to determine your capital gain rate.

The capital gain income tax rate is lower than your ordinary income tax rate. For instance, if your joint ordinary income is less than

$80,000 (the top of the 12% tax band), then your capital gain rate is 0%. If it is not over $500,000, then instead of paying the ordinary tax of 32% on your capital gains, you would pay 15%. However, your capital gains act like a float to not only tax your ordinary income at a higher rate, but also to determine what your capital gain rate is going to be.

Take for instance the person whose ordinary income is $80,000 and has $20,000 of capital gain income. Great! $80,000 is taxed at 12% and the tax on the capital gain is 0%. Not so fast! To determine the capital gain rate, you must add the capital gain income to the ordinary income. That is $100,000 meaning your capital gain rate is really 15%. Then, the capital gain income is used as the foundation of your ordinary tax calculation using up the first $20,000 of the tax bands, which floats $20,000 of your ordinary income up into the 22% band of income. This is the true definition of, "they've got you coming and going".

It happens again when you have extraordinary income from the sale of an investment property. In this situation, what you do not know may be more important than what you do know. We know that any gain in a capital asset is taxed at capital gain rates, but did you know that when you sell a depreciable investment property, all the depreciation must be "recaptured" as ordinary income on top of the capital gain? I find the novice real estate investor does not know this until it happens, when it is too late.

If you sell a fully depreciated property for $120,000 that originally cost $100,000, that means you have a $20,000 capital gain and a $100,000 recapture of depreciation as income. Tax float from this transaction moves all your other taxable income up by $120,000.

Since the 22% tax band starts at approximately $80,000, you can see how the real estate transaction forces your ordinary earned income into a higher band.

If you did not know that depreciation must be recaptured, I am 99.9% confident you did not know the impact of tax float either. That is unless this has happened to you before. If you do not prepare your own income tax returns, you will unknowingly suffer this consequence of tax float repeatedly.

The fourth misperception that I would like to address is the concept of tax compounding. A deferred tax is never the tax paid in the future. If tax rates in the future stay the same, the tax paid in the future will always be more than the tax not paid today. That is because you are the government's best investor. Because you have not paid the tax when due, you merely deferred it, the unpaid tax is commingled as part of the entire investment. When your investment goes up, your unpaid debt to the government, goes up as well. If your investment goes down, so does what you owe the government. But, in the long term, we observe that a well-diversified portfolio goes up. When we do better, the government does better. Isn't it interesting that when the investment markets move drastically down, the government suspends the required minimum distribution of older Americans? This happened in 2008 and again in 2020. Why would the government require you to make a transaction that will lose the government money? They allow you to keep what you owe them, invested along with your share of the account, so that the government can recover from the market loss before reinstating the requirement to withdraw a portion of the account and pay your taxes. They fully embrace the slogan "we do better when you do better". This is proof that what is reported as your money in your IRA or 401(k) is not really all yours. Some is yours and some is theirs. How the government might look at your untaxed money in the future may be discovered when you combine the two words, "The IRS".

Even though your retirement plan statement only includes your name at the top, it is not all yours. Inside is a tax debt to the federal government and to the state government. How much is theirs and how much is yours is determined when you want to use the money. I am confident that your retirement plan charges fees on the account. Do you pay investment fees on only the part that is yours, or do you pay fees on the entire account? Not only does the IRS get to collect on your tax debt at whatever rate they want to charge, but they also get you to pay the investment fees on their money.

The fifth misperception to address is how our government plays the "hidden object trick" on us. A magician will always offer some form of distraction to divert your attention from their real objective. Maybe the magician's trick is to make a dollar bill disappear right in front of your eyes. All they must do is get you to look elsewhere.

There is a difference between tax rates and tax thresholds. Tax rates get all the publicity, but the tax thresholds are where all the power to tax exists. When an administration wants to either raise or lower income taxes, all that is reported are the potential rates. Rates are the distraction. Behind the scenes the tax experts are working the real magic, with the thresholds. President Ronald Reagan was a master at this.

When Reagan wanted to stimulate the economy, he advocated reducing the rate. Everyone was on board. In 1980, when Reagan became President, the top tax rate was 70% on incomes over $215,000.

Reagan campaigned on and fulfilled his campaign promises by reducing the top tax rate to 50%. But the tax revenues rose by $19 billion. Up when the rates went down? That is because behind the scenes the top tax threshold, the amount of income upon which the top rate is applied was reduced from $215,000 to $85,000. The sleight of hand occurred when the top tax rate of 50% was applied to income levels whose previous rate was less than 50%. It worked so well, Reagan did it again in 1987 and again in 1988 when he got the top tax rate down to 28%. But the top threshold was reduced to $29,000. By 1988, most Americans were paying the top tax rate.

Beware, as we progress through the 21st century, and the National Debt grows, we must eventually address paying the debt as well ongoing public expenditures. Will we need to increase the tax rates and reduce the tax thresholds at the same time? At least Reagan dropped both the rate and thresholds at the same time. Roosevelt is the example in our history when he raised the rate and lowered the thresholds at the same time.

3

Rate of Return

"Common sense is in spite of, not as the result of education."
Victor Hugo

"I mean, you could claim that anything's real, if the only basis
for believing in it
is that nobody's proved it doesn't exist!"
J.K. Rowling,
Harry Potter and the Deathly Hallows

What is average? Something average is either common or typical. When used to describe a rate of return, it is what can be expected to happen repeatedly. It either provides a simplistic report of the past or a hypothetical projection of the future. Expectations of the future are often based on what happened in the past, even though every investment projection you see states that "past performance is not a prediction of future expectations." A common way of looking at averages is to calculate the mean of a series of numbers. The mean return over several years is the sum of the returns during those specific years, divided by the number of years you are looking at. This number is commonly referred to as the average rate of return. However you define "average," I've learned that what I've been taught about averages couldn't be further from the actual truth.

Let us start with a simple example. If you had $1,000 and averaged 20% return per year for two years, you would expect to have $1,440 at the conclusion of two years.

An average rate of return is a simplistic and convenient way to project the future potential of a financial plan. Too bad it does not work. The main reason why average rates of return are a faulty way of looking at your finances is because averages are not what you earn, and the order in which actual returns occur can make a big difference.

Take, for example, the S&P 500 index for the period 1973 through 1997. During this 25-year time period, the S&P suffered through some of its worst periods of time, including a single-day drop of over 22% in 1987, and one of its longest rallies during the 1990s. During this time period, the index had an average annual rate of return of 10.11%. Indeed, if you added up each individual annual return and divided by 25, you would arrive at the statistical average of 10.11%. (Source: www.standardandpoors.com)

If you invested $100,000 in 1973 and actually earned 10.11% each year for 25 years, you would have the expectation that your nest egg would be $1,110,000. Unfortunately, you do not earn the same rate each year. Let us calculate what you would have actually had at the conclusion of those 25 years if you had invested $100,000 in 1973 and earned what the market actually earned year after year. If you had left it to grow and compound, you would have $821,000. This is a difference of $279,000 less than the average would have created! A 25% loss when you compare your expectations with reality, just because we were not taught correctly.

Lesson #1: What I was taught to be true about rates of return that has turned out not to be true, is that averages are not what you actually get to spend and enjoy.

If the actual returns between 1973 through 1997 are inverted, so that the actual return in 1973 is assumed to have occurred in 1997 and vice versa, for each year, the average is still 10.11%. However, the actual account value of the $100,000 invested over that 25-year period is now, $792,000. The order in which you earn the actual rate of return matters.

The simple randomness of your actual returns in this example cost you $29,000. Another negative blow to reality, just because we are not taught correctly.

Lesson #2: What I was taught to be true about rates of return that has turned out not to be true, is that the order in which you actually earn the rate of return matters. Further emphasizing that average rates of return have nothing to do with your eventual account balance.

The coincidence of updating this book 10 years later is that the update has come during the Covid-19 pandemic of 2020. The sudden drop in the investment market further illustrates the impact of misunderstanding rates of return.

The 20-year period, 2000 through 2019, is a period that looks remarkably like the period just examined. Because of the large positive and negative swings of the market, the average rate of return during that time was 7.68% in the S&P 500 index including dividends. The last 12 years of this 20-year period, the total return of the S&P was over 300%. The average of less than 8%, logically seems low. It is not, that is the right number. Sometimes our heads get in the way of reality as much as mathematical averages. The actual return during this period is 6.06%. That is over 1.6 percentage points less than the average. Be careful thinking that it is 1.6% less. It is 1.6 percentage points less, which is actually 21% lower than the average. That is the reality.

Lesson #3: What I was taught to be true about rates of return that has turned out not to be true, is that you must differentiate between a percentage point difference and percentage rate difference.

As if this were not bad enough, factor in the first 2 ½ months of 2020, just as the economic impact of Covid-19 hit the U. S. Equity markets. Factoring in the S&P 500 loss of 28.5% during the period January 1, 2020 through March 22, 2020, the actual 20 year and 3-month annual return falls to 4.3%. That is 44% less than what averages would lead you to believe.

What did it take to get back to the January 1, 2020 balances? Not 28%. You always must earn more than you lose percentagewise to get back to your original account balance. Averages will tell you that if you lose 28% in one year, all you must do is earn 28% the next year. -28% + 28% = 0%. That is math. No loss, back to where you started. Not true! What will it really take to get back to the same dollar value you had on January 1? 40%! -28% + 40% = 0%. That is reality.

If you had $1,000 on January 1, after the Covid-19 loss of 28% you now have $720. If you leave the $720 invested and it regains 28% you only have $921. Only if you earn 40% on your remaining $720 will you get back to $1,000.

Lesson #4: What I was taught to be true about rates of return that has turned out not to be true, is that you must earn more than you lose just to break even. The reality is that in the investment markets, losses are always subtracted from higher account values and gains are always added to lower account values.

From what we learned in Chapters 1 and 2, what hasn't been accounted for yet? That is right, taxes. Average rates of return— in fact, actual returns as well—are never reduced for taxes when they are disclosed to you. Those typical mountain charts that you are provided, every time you purchase a mutual fund assumes you are paying the taxes on the growth of the fund out of your pocket, from your lifestyle.

Let us apply Lesson # 4 from the Compound Interest chapter. What if the taxes due were netted out of the account instead of out of your standard of living? Let us consider a hypothetical mutual fund that had a 76-year history by 2010. Without netting the taxes out of the fund balance, the marketing piece would show that $10,000 invested in the fund in 1934 would grow to almost $58.5 million if you reinvested the dividends paid by the fund, by 2010. The marketing materials never indicate that the taxes due each year on the growth of the fund were paid by the investor's "other" money to make the numbers and graph work. If you netted an assumed 30% ordinary tax rate and 15% capital gain rate from the fund, your $10,000 investment 76 years ago would be just shy of $8.9 million to-day. That is 84% less than what you are led to believe from the fund's growth chart.

Lesson #5: What I was taught to be true about rates of return that has turned out not to be true, is that taxes are never considered when calculating my account balance and they take a large portion of actual rate of return away.

Now that you have a good feel for why what we are taught about rates of return is not necessarily true, let us finish with the simple example we started with. By now, you are probably thinking that what seems to be simple may not be. Our example was that an investment of $1,000 that averages 20% over two years would yield $1,440. But might it also yield the following:

$1,280? It sure will. An extremely volatile market that earns 60% in the first year and then loses 20% the second year has an average rate of return of 20% but an account value of $1,280, not $1,440.

$800? How can you average a positive rate of return and end up with less money? In the real estate boom and bust of the late 2000's, you could purchase an unbuilt home and sell it for twice what you paid for it before you moved in. That is a 100% return. Shortly thereafter, that same property fell 60% in value. Over the two-year period, the average rate of return was 20%, yet you have less money than you started with.

$0? Now you know this is a trick question, but again it is true. You can average 20% for two years and yet lose all your money. Anyone who earns 140% and then loses it all—that is, 100%—ends up with $0, and yet averages 20%.

Lesson #6: What I was taught to be true about rates of return that has turned out not to be true is that how much money you end up with is more important than any rate of return. Advertised or stated rates have been far different from what I have experienced.

4

Paper Gains

"Success is more a function of consistent common sense than it is of genius."
Dr. An Wang

"The same principles which at first view lead to skepticism, pursued to a certain point, bring men back to common sense."
George Berkeley

You may have heard a friend or overheard someone in a crowd tell everyone about their trip to Las Vegas and how they hit the $16,000 jackpot. It was awesome!

Everybody is just fascinated and wishes they had been there to experience the thrill, right? Sure, it is exciting. No wonder they are building casinos all over the country, so more and more people can experience the same high.

Many of you have experienced those same highs when you open your quarterly investment statements. No matter, what the statement says, the fact is that you had no gain or loss at all, because you did not cash out at the time the statement was printed. We call those "paper gains," or "paper losses" because those gains or losses are worth no more or less than the paper they were printed on, that is unless you call your adviser and have them move that money out of what they are invested in and realize those gains or losses. The paper gains reported at the end of 1999 were lost in 2000 – 2002 and were not recovered until 2007, only to be lost again in 2008. Then, it took until 2012 to regain those losses so that you had the same account value as you did in 1999. Over this 12-year period, that is an actual rate of return of .55% per year. You could have done better in a savings account even though at various points in time your statements showed that you had doubled your money. Doubling your money happened between 2000 – 2002, and again 2003 – 2007, if you were invested in the S&P 500 index. Those gains were never yours; they were just paper gains.

Lesson #1: What I was taught to be true about our investment statements that has turned out not to be true, is that even though your name is at the top of the statement the money is not necessarily yours. Not until you lock in the values and cash them out.

Do you ever wonder why your investment provider sends you a statement showing you how much money is in your IRA or 401(k)? Why report what you cannot have? The penalty for early withdrawal of your IRA is 10% of what you take out prior to age 59 ½. The investment provider does not show that. The penalty for early withdrawal of your 401(k) is much more severe. Not only do you have a 10% penalty if you are not age 59 ½, but you also must terminate your employment to get the funds that are reported to you each quarter. Because you have not terminated your employment, the value (that which you can actually use) of your account is really $0. By the time you are eligible to withdraw your funds after you terminate your employment, what is reported at age 50 will not have any relationship to what you have access to at age 60. Hopefully, it is more, but it could be less. So why bother with the interim statements?

Just think of those who retired on February 18, 2020. The paper statement said they had earned 401% since March 9, 2009. They had hit the jackpot. Retirement was theirs. If their February 18, 2020 account balance was $1,000,000, just one month later, the statement showed an account balance of only $700,000. Back to work? The $1,000,000 paper gain was not really theirs, it was just paper wealth, unless they locked in the paper gain and cashed it out.

The same goes for real estate, precious metals, or crypto currency, or wherever the flavor-of-the-week "jackpot" happens to be that quarter. By 2008, many had supposedly doubled or tripled the price they had paid for their home. These gains were not even reported on paper, but they were in our minds. However, we could not put our hands on it.

There are companies spending fortunes advertising gold and silver as the next "jackpot" just waiting to be taken by the highest bidder. Even though you may have those shiny little coins locked up in your safe in the basement, the metal is only worth the price on the paper advertising the latest bid price.

Lesson #2: What I was taught to be true about our investment statements, our gold bricks, or our houses that has turned out not to be true, is that when you hear that someone, somewhere, somehow sold their house for that unbelievable price, that must mean yours is worth that much as well. You may also find out that when you decide it is time to cash out, your home, gold or your 401(k), it does not have the actual value your statement said it once had.

Another problem with paper gains is that the account statements never show any taxes due on the account value. Whether you have a tax deferred retirement account, or an after-tax investment account; you have partners. Partners? Yes, unfortunately, your paper statement does not show how much your federal, state, and local governments want first. Taxes due never show up on the statement because the actual stake your partners take is not disclosed until the day you try to take some of the money for yourself. At that time, these governments decide how much they want first, leaving you with whatever is left.

Lesson #3: What I was taught to be true about our investment statements, that has turned out not to be true, is that it is not all mine. My partners determine how much they want first, then I get what is left.

Our paper gains lead to a false sense of security, as lifestyle purchases are based on the paper gain, not the actual economic value of the realizable gains. During the stock market boom of the 1980s and 1990s, many people transferred safe funds to the market to participate in these gains. Consumer purchases were made along the way without a responsible transfer of the paper gains back to safe money, only to see the paper gains disappear in the early 2000s and again in 2008. If you are going to spend the market's paper gains, you must systematically and responsibly turn the paper gains into realized gains.

Lesson #4: What I was taught to be true about paper gains that has turned out not to be true, is that paper gains have no purchasing power. Just try taking your February 18, 2020 statement and ask for its value one month later. You will only get 70% of what the paper says.

BRYAN S. BLOOM

5

Be A Long Term Investor

"Nothing astonishes men so much as common sense and plain dealing."
Ralph Waldo Emerson

"The three great essentials to achieve anything worthwhile are:
Hard work, Stick-to-itiveness,
and Common sense."
Thomas A. Edison

A second cousin to the average rate of return rule that we learn is the long-term investment rule. If you are a long-term investor, you can ignore the day-to-day volatility of the market. Stock market history shows that the market has a long-term upward slope of increasing returns. We are often pointed to the mountain charts discussed in the "Rate of Return" chapter.

The history of the S&P 500 proves this well. Just look at the following long-term average rates of return:

	Average	Actual	Nominal Difference By Percentage	Actual Difference By Percentage
1940-2019	12.42%	11.06%	-1.36%	-12.30%
1950-2019	12.74%	11.35%	-1.39%	-12.20%
1960-2019	11.41%	10.08%	-1.33%	-13.20%
1970-2019	11.97%	10.55%	-1.42%	-13.50%
1980-2019	13.11%	11.78%	-1.33%	-11.30%
1990-2019	11.45%	9.96%	-1.49%	-15.00%
2000-2019	7.68%	6.06%	-1.62%	-26.70%
2000-March 2020	5.96%	4.30%	-1.66%	-38.60%

(Source: www.standardandpoors.com)

As long as you are looking at a time span of around twenty years or more, you would think you will eventually get an average 11-12% return on your money. We were told that the 9/11 terrorist attack on the United States, would change what we once knew to be true. Life would never be the same. Perhaps, the most recent 20-year period is an indication of the "new normal" long term rate of return. The investor must decide. If this dramatic effect disturbs you, seek out the expertise of someone who knows the difference between money and wealth as described in the other books in the series, Confessions of a CPA.

As we have already learned, we must not count on the averages, because average is not what you get, but instead, actual year-to-year returns. You can still amass a small fortune in the long term as long as you pay the taxes from your lifestyle.

However, these are not the returns that the average investor receives. The 2019 Dalbar Study of Investor Returns found that over the 20 years ending in 2018, when the S&P 500 returned an average of 5.6% (S&P 500 Index without dividends), the average equity investor earned just 3.88%. The study also revealed that in 2018 alone, the average investor lost 9.4% while the S&P 500 only lost 4.4%; more than twice as much. (Source: www.dalbar.com.)

Why is that? Part of it is investment selection, but most of the difference is allocated to investor behavior. The 2018 difference was attributed to "the average investor took some money off the table in 2018 but was still poorly positioned for the second half of the year." Investors just do not buy and hold for the long term. They tend to get in the market near its high, because as the market is going up, it seems safe. Part of it is also that they do not want to be left out of the party, so they join their friends and invest. Alan Greenspan, the former Federal Reserve chairman, has referred to this as "irrational exuberance." Then, when the market corrects, they exercise some control and stay in, understanding that they are long-term investors. When they begin to see others get out of the market, they start to lose sleep, and they sell near the bottom of the correction. Then, as the market begins to recover, they wait, they vow they are not going to be caught by a "sucker's rally," wait a little more, make sure the market is really back on the upward climb, and then get back in. They literally buy high and sell low, only to buy high again! The human psyche is more fragile than the computer models that can calculate the long-term rates of return we all ought to be getting if we are just patient.

Notice also that the long term is a long time. The money must be in the market to get these returns. You cannot chicken out and you cannot spend the money, not even to pay the taxes due on the growth.

Lesson #1: What I was taught to be true about being a long-term investor that has turned out not to be true is that being a long-term investor requires a discipline or stubbornness that human behavior patterns rarely allow.

When my daughter, a graduate of one of the most highly rated public universities in America, started her career in finance it was just in time to see the stock market fall by 40% and then quickly rebound by 50%. She called on the phone and told me that she had a training presentation to give, and she just could not get the numbers to work out; would I help her? She explained that she wanted to show how well the market had recovered from its recent collapse. She used the example of $100,000 invested in this volatile 40% down and-50% up market. She quickly discovered that what she was taught to be true turned out not to be. Rates of return are not additive. And even though the premise of the previous chapter on averages would lead you to believe that over the two years you had earned 10% total, 5% average, it was not just not true; it wasn't even close.

$100,000
less 40% the market "correction"
=$60,000

plus 50% the market "recovery"
=$90,000

I confirmed with her that her numbers were right, and instead of earning an average 5% over the two-year period, she actually lost an average 5% per year.

Then she made a remarkable statement that led to this chapter. She said, "just think if you didn't lose money. If the 40% loss could have just been a break-even year, then even if I just earned half of what the market earned the next year, I'd have $125,000."

Let us see how our long-term rates of return would have fared if we could eliminate all the negatives, replace them with zeros, and take just 75% of the positives. For each of the following time periods below, you would have the stated rate of return over and above what staying in the market for the long term would have yielded.

	Average	75% of the "up" 0% of the "down"
1940–2019	12.42%	15.85%
1950–2019	12.74%	16.00%
1960–2019	11.41%	14.87%
1970–2019	11.97%	15.34%
1980–2019	13.11%	15.85%
1990–2019	11.45%	14.79%
2000–2019	7.68%	12.28%
2010-2019	14.15%	14.85%

(Source: www.standardandpoors.com)

Here is another way to look at this. If you invested $10,000 at the beginning of each of these periods, by eliminating the negatives of the stock market but only taking 80% of the gain when the market went up, your investment nest egg would be higher in every period of time.

	All the Return	Eliminating the Losses	More Money	Percent More
1940-2019	44,092,000	63,417,900	19,325,900	43%
1950-2019	18,508,300	24,256,500	5,748,200	31%
1960-2019	3,185,400	5,161,300	1,975,900	62%
1970-2019	150,960	222,740	71,780	47%
1980-2019	86,150	90,500	4,350	5%
1990-2019	17,270	23,350	6,080	35%
2000-2019	3,240	5,790	2,550	78%

This table illustrates that small advantages can mean a lot of money in real terms in the long run. For instance, the advantage of limiting the gains to only 80% in exchange for eliminating all the losses is only a 5% difference during the period 1980–2019, which does not sound like much. But that is a real dollar advantage of over $4,350.

Lesson #2: What I was taught to be true about being a long-term investor that has turned out not to be true, is that even in a buy and hold strategy, volatility does not smooth out. Taking unlimited losses with the unlimited gains may be a losing strategy. Limit your losses, even at the expense of some of your gains.

One of the longest-standing traditional investment strategies is dollar cost averaging; that is, getting into the market a little at a time. If you invest the same amount of money on a regular basis as the market is going up, your invested total grows systematically as you add money. You merely purchase fewer, more valuable individual shares. However, you limit your upside potential since you didn't buy all at once at the low price. At the same time, you are protecting your available investment dollars should the market move down unexpectedly.

If the market heads lower, you still invest the same amount of money, but you buy more shares at a lower price. You are never buying your entire position either high or low. Dollar cost averaging helps your discipline to stay invested in the declining market, because you are systematically buying more less expensive shares. You continue to buy and to stay invested.

Rarely is it spoken of to "dollar cost average" out of the market. If you a look at the ten years, 1999–2008, you find that you would have been better off taking principal out during the downturn (limiting your loss of principal) and taking gains out during the upturn (protecting what the market gave you). Here is a simple example of removing 5% of your initial investment over this ten-year period.

This first chart shows the results had you left the money in the market over the entire period. (Source: www.standardand-poors.com.) An initial investment of $100,000 would have been worth $73,461 ten years later.

	Rate of Return	Beginning of the Year	Gain or Loss	End of the Year
1999	19.51%	100,000	19,510	119,510
2000	-10.14%	119,510	-12,118	107,392
2001	-13.04%	107,392	-14,004	93,388
2002	-23.37%	93,388	-21,825	71,563
2003	26.38%	71,563	18,878	90,441
2004	8.99%	90,441	8,131	98,572
2005	3.00%	98,572	2,957	101,529
2006	13.62%	101,529	13,828	115,358
2007	3.53%	115,358	4,072	119,430
2008	-38.49%	119,430	-45,968	73,461

What if you had exercised the strategy of dollar cost averaging yourself out of the market, as outlined above, and removed 5% of the original investment ($5,000) each year? The growth chart would look like this:

By stripping off a percentage of the account each year, you would end up with $36,564 plus the $50,000 you stripped off, resulting in a total of $86,564. If you had just left the money in the account because you are a long-term investor, you would have $73,461, a difference of $13,103. This difference assumes you stuck the $5,000 each year into a mattress for safekeeping. Perhaps the money ought to land in an account that can be safe, secure, and tax-free to avoid the pitfalls of traditional thinking that we have already discovered.

Lesson #3: What I was taught to be true about being a long-term investor that has turned out not to be true, is that leaving all your eggs in one basket, taking the downs with the ups, may not be any better than systematically removing risk from your investments by retreating to tax-free safety.

6

Qualified Plans

"Common sense will tell us, that the power which hath endeav-
ored to subdue us, is of all others,
the most improper to defend us."
Thomas Paine

"The problem is that agencies sometimes lose sight of common
sense as they create regulations."
Fred Thompson

A qualified plan is any arrangement offered by your employer in which the government provides a tax deduction for making an investment. It allows the tax on the growth of the account to be postponed to an uncertain date at an uncertain rate. A qualified plan is commonly known as a 401(k), 403(b), 457, or SEP plan. Since an IRA is not offered by employers, it is technically not a qualified plan, but in many ways acts like a qualified plan. Not only do you get the miracle of compound interest working in your favor, but you also do not have to pay the tax, until you take the money out of the plan.

The employer plans offer a vast but limited array of investment choices, anywhere from aggressive growth funds to stable value funds. The funds allowed for investment by your employer must include investment choices spread out over the spectrum of risk. You are not required to put a set amount in any one fund. The money you put into one of these employer plans is always yours, but sometimes you must meet certain criteria to access your money. Some of those requirements may include attaining a certain age, terminating your employment, or suffering a government-defined hardship.

Some employers sweeten the opportunity for you to participate. The enticement sounds like this: "If you put your money in, we (the employer) will put some in as well." The amount put in by the employer is defined by the employer. It is subject to government mandated testing for discrimination against the lower-paid employees, and it may be subject to other criteria. Some of these requirements include working a minimum number of hours each year or being employed on the last day of the year. Most of the time, employer contributions are subject to a vesting schedule. Vesting represents how much of the employer money is yours. Typically, the longer your tenure at your employer, the more of the employer's money becomes yours. If you do not stay employed, all or a portion of the employer contributions made to your account is forfeited. The money the employer puts into the plan is tax-deductible for the employer, much like general compensation is, and can grow tax deferred. Because the employer receives a tax deduction and the money in the account grows tax deferred, all the money is taxable to the employee when it is withdrawn.

An IRA is an individual retirement account that you can set up for yourself if you are not a member of an employer-qualified plan. You get a tax deduction for the money you put in, and it grows tax deferred. Employer-qualified plans can be consolidated with IRA accounts where the employer money is made available to you through a process called a trustee-to-trustee transfer or rollover. Investment opportunities available in an IRA are virtually limitless.

What makes these arrangements so attractive?

1. You do not have to pay current income taxes on the money as it is added to the account.
2. You do not have to pay current income taxes on the growth of the money each year.
3. You are investing by "dollar cost averaging". You are buying more shares when the price of the investment is low and buying fewer shares when the price is high, consequently averaging out the cost of participating in the plan.
4. You are taking advantage of the miracle of compound interest. Because this is a retirement plan, there are serious restrictions to accessing the money during your employment. From a previous chapter, we have learned that it takes time for the miracle to take shape, so it has a real possibility to work in this

situation, since access is restricted over your career. This gives you a 30 to 40-year investment timeframe.Your investment is being made as a payroll deduction; therefore, you hardly notice the money is gone. What you do not see, you do not spend.

5. We are taught to save for retirement systematically, because a little sacrifice now will provide a great benefit later. If you can get your employer to add their money to yours, that is like getting free money. Because it grows tax deferred, it becomes a powerful retirement savings tool. A qualified plan is one of the most explosive accumulation tools available to most employees.

It is hard to argue with all these benefits. However, it is these very advantages that contribute to making these plans erosive to your wealth when you need it the most, in your retirement years. When you begin to peel back the layers, like an onion, it begins to smell! You discover that what we have been taught to be true, is not true at all and may be one of the worst hoaxes ever perpetrated on the American worker.

Let us look at what I was taught to be true about qualified plans, and what I have discovered over years of practical experience, is not true.

First, I was taught that we are saving taxes by putting money into a qualified plan.

If you were to go to the bank and ask the banker for a loan, and they said your loan was approved, what two questions would you want an answer to before you accepted the money? You would want to know what interest rate the bank was going to charge and when the bank wanted the money back. What if the banker told you that at the present time, the bank had plenty of money and does not need the money back right away? In fact, you could keep the money until the bank needed it, and at that point the bank would determine the interest rate retroactive to the origination of the loan. Would you take the bank's money? Of course not!

That bank loan example is similar to what we are doing when we participate in a tax deferred qualified plan. The IRS is due the income taxes on the income we earn, as we earn it, with a few exceptions. One of the exceptions is money we put into a qualified plan. The taxes that would otherwise be due on the money we put into the qualified plan are deferred until some uncertain time. For the most part, we oversee when we pay these taxes, as we use the qualified plan money as income in retirement. However, the IRS demands that we begin paying the taxes at age 72. Could the IRS change the required minimum distribution age? Sure they could. They have changed it three times since the required minimum was included in the scheme established by Congress in 1974. Originally, the age was 70 ½, then in 2008 it was eliminated for a year. The age of 70 ½ was reestablished after the economy recovered from the 2008 market crash, then was changed in 2020 to 72. Shortly after the effects of Covid-19 became apparent in March 2020, the requirement was suspended again and has been reestablished as of January 1, 2021 back to 72. The taxes we defer are like taking a loan from the IRS for money that the IRS is otherwise due today and agreeing to pay it back according to the IRS's schedule and at the income tax rate in effect at that time. Could the IRS forgive the tax "loan"? Sure it could. Could the IRS assess a tax rate higher or lower than the tax rate that was in effect when the taxes were deferred? Sure it could. Could the IRS assess a "success" tax on qualified plan balances over a certain amount that it might believe to be excessive? Sure it could. Which do you think is a more likely outcome? Tax forgiveness? A lower future tax rate? A higher future tax rate? An excise tax? When we participate in a qualified plan, we are agreeing to pay these taxes otherwise due today, at some uncertain date, at some uncertain rate. Would you agree to that with your banker?

Of course not.

Lesson #1: What I was taught to be true about qualified plans that has turned out not to be true, is that qualified plans do not save taxes. They merely defer or postpone the tax to some uncertain date, at some uncertain rate. Qualified plans do not avoid income taxes; they merely put them off until later.

So, we defer the tax; what is the big deal? It is just a word. Some say, "If I put $5,000 into a deductible IRA, and I am in the 25% tax bracket, I save the payment of $1,250. I will just pay it later, because I can earn interest on the $1,250, I don't pay today." Let us think about that.

If this were your plan for thirty years, you would have put aside $150,000, and you would have deferred $37,500 of income taxes. If that account were invested and received an average 8% return each year, your retirement account would be worth $611,729. If you chose to supplement your other retirement income with this money for twenty years in retirement, at 8% you could withdraw $57,691 per year before you would run out of money. This is what I mean about being taught that this is one of the most explosive accumulation tools of all time. If you started paying the $1,250 that you did not pay in taxes when you were adding money to the account, from this retirement cash flow, you would net out $56,441. "Big deal!" you say. "That is still a large sum of money to supplement my other retirement income."

But it does not work that way! You do not just pay back what you deferred. You pay back an amount equal to the tax rate in the year you withdraw it, and it is assessed against the entire amount you withdraw. If you are still in the 25% tax bracket, your annual tax bill will be $14,423 each year for twenty years. That is $288,425 in taxes paid during your withdrawal years. So much for saving taxes! In fact, the taxes saved, $37,500, are paid in less than three years of retirement. Even though you have paid the government all the taxes deferred from your contributions, you get to keep paying them to cover all of the taxes deferred on what the entire investment earned. You pay taxes not only on the growth attributed to the portion of the account that is yours, but also on the portion that will go to the IRS.

To add insult to injury, if you withdraw an amount that exceeds a government mandated amount, your withdrawal will subject your Social Security payments to income taxes. If you can stay under the amount that the government dictates, your Social Security will be tax-free. It makes you wonder who really owns these accounts!

Some choose to leave the money in the qualified plan and not use it. You cannot do that either! The government wants its money! Beginning at age 72, you are supposed to know the amount you must take out each year. If you do not get it right, only then will the government tell you what you should have taken out. They will then access the income tax due on what you should have taken out and add a penalty of 50% of what should have been taken out. Then you get to have the same conversation with your State IRS. After your retirement partners take their share, that does not leave much for you!

Some choose to take out only what they must and leave the rest for their children at their death. That does not work either. Your adult age children get to pay the tax, at their tax rate. Perhaps that is at the height of their best earning years. They are forced to pay the tax over the 10 years after your death. If you leave a sizable, qualified plan balance as an inheritance, you can imagine what 10% of that value every year for 10 years will do to their personal income tax bracket? Uncle Sam always gets its money. When we leave a qualified plan as an inheritance, we not only leave the account value as an inheritance but also a tax bill. Thanks, Mom and Dad!

Lesson #2: What I was taught to be true about qualified plans that has turned out not to be true, is that while some describe these arrangements as tax free because you do not pay the current income taxes on the amount put into the plan, they are far from tax free. Not only do you owe the tax you did not pay but also what those taxes earned while they were in your account. If your share went up, so did the government's. As your account compounds, your income tax debt compounds as well.

Another lesson in the above example is that not only do qualified plans defer the tax, but they also defer the tax calculation. The tax rate you would have paid had you not participated in the qualified plan may or may not be the rate you will pay when the taxes are due. It is just like letting the banker set the interest rate on a loan retroactively.

Lesson #3: What I was taught to be true about qualified plans that has turned out not to be true, is that qualified plans not only defer the taxes, but they also defer the tax calculation. What you owe in retirement taxes will be exponentially more than you defer, even if the rate does not change. The tax you do not pay compounds, and the rate at which the debt accrues is not determined until the IRS decides how much of it they want.

Do you think tax rates are going to go up in the future, go down in the future, or stay the same? Consider that Social Security is going broke, Medicare is on life support, the Pension Benefit Guaranty Corporation is out of money, and the cost of the Covid-19 virus response being added to the National Debt. Will that be $2 trillion? $4 trillion? It appears that the Covid-19 cost in the U.S. will exceed $7 trillion. Our National Debt will be more than $30,000,000,000,000! Here is a snapshot of the debt clock, just as the Covid-19 virus was becoming a reality:

www.usdebtclock.org April 5, 2020

Here is the National Debt Clock as of August 22, 2021. Focus on the top left number. That is our National Debt. It has increased over 20% in a matter of 16 months. See what I mean about the Covid-19 relief being added to our national debt?

www.usdebtclock.org August 22, 2021

How do you think we are going to get out of this?

As you read this section, stop and look at the usdebtclock.org website and see what it has increased to now.

At the end of the third quarter of 2018, the Federal Reserve reported that U.S. Citizens owned retirement assets in excess of $26,500,000,000,000. (Source: https://www.federalreserve.gov) Yes, that is right, equal to our current National Debt. If the U. S. Government can set tax policy whenever and at whatever level they choose in the future, have you ever wondered why there is not much discussion about the National Debt?

Today, we already have an extra tax on social security, if your income exceeds $25,000 as a single taxpayer and $34,000 if you are a married couple. Could there be a separate tax someday, just on your qualified plan?

Not only is there pressure for general income tax brackets to go up, but your personal income tax rate may go up as well, because:

- you have paid off your home mortgage, consequently losing the tax deduction associated with home mortgage interest.
- your children have exceeded the age at which you receive a child tax credit.
- by the time you are retired, your children are no longer dependents and are no longer qualified for personal exemptions on your tax return (these exemptions were suspended until 2026, when they are scheduled to be restored).

Lessons #4: What I was taught to be true about qualified plans that has turned out not to be true, is that you probably will not retire in a lower tax bracket. On top of paying taxes at whatever tax rate the IRS determines the rate to be at the time you must pay the tax, your personal circumstances will impact the eventual rate as well.

We were also taught that we will retire in a lower tax bracket than when we were working. That might be true if you are saving for retirement truly tax free, but as discussed, these qualified plans are anything but tax free. If all your retirement income comes from a tax deferred source like a qualified plan, a successful retirement means that you are merely trading your taxable paycheck for a taxable IRA distribution.

Another principle we were taught was that you can retire on 70% of your pre-retirement income.

Lessons #5: What I was taught to be true about qualified plans that has turned out not to be true, is that a 70% income goal is a goal you set in order to fail. I have yet to see anyone able to live on 70% of what they cannot live on today.

To be comfortable in retirement, you must have complete replacement of your pre-retirement income, or part of your retirement plan must include part time retirement employment or living with your children.

The last lesson about qualified plans we are going to talk about is ownership. Just because your name is on your quarterly plan statement does not mean that the money is yours. First, you must meet the vesting requirements of your employer to claim ownership of the employer's matching contributions. Even after that, the account is not yours. Because of taxation, the government has first claim on your account. How many government agencies want a piece of the pie? Do not forget your state needs money as well as your city. After the taxes are paid, at whatever the rate is in the future, the rest is finally yours. Could the government raise the tax rate in the future? Could it raise the tax on just qualified plans to something greater than the normal tax rate? Could it reinstate the old excess withdrawal tax, or institute a windfall elimination tax on qualified plans? I will leave the answer to you, but these are uncertainties that can cause sleepless nights.

As you withdraw money from your qualified plan to live on, who else is waiting in the wings for their share? Social Security sets an income test to determine whether your Social Security payments are taxable. If your qualified plan distribution is "too much", then the government will tax what you receive from Social Security. Medicare also tests your income to determine the premium you will pay for Medicare. In 1966, the initial Medicare premium was $3 per month per person. In 2021, that has risen to $148.50 per month per person. Unless you have too much income. Even if that income comes from your retirement nest egg. The Medicare income-based premium could force you to pay as much as $582 per month per person.

Lesson #6: What I was taught to be true about qualified plans that has turned out not to be true, is that the government has the first claim on the distributions from all qualified plans; I get the portion the government does not take away in taxes and surcharges first.

Qualified plans may be the most efficient method of accumulating money for retirement, but they can be the most inefficient when you need the money the most.

7

Buy Term And Invest The Rest

"Common sense is the measure of the possible; it is composed of
experience and prevision;
it is calculation applied to life."
Henri Frederic Amiel

"Common sense is instinct, and enough of it is genius."
Josh Billings

Life insurance is often considered a necessary evil: something you pay for and never receive. Life insurance is designed to help a family financially if the income earner meets with an early demise. The question you must ask yourself is what would your dependents do if you were to die? In this sense, life insurance ought to be labeled death insurance.

Some might say, "my spouse will remarry"; others will say, "they will get a job, or a second job." Others will say, "if I buy enough life insurance, they will not have to do either. My family may have to move ahead without me, but they will do so without a financial hardship."

If you settle on the last response, then you must decide which kind of life insurance is best. There are many choices. One of the most popular is to buy enough term life insurance to cover your most financially exposed years and then invest the difference between the inexpensive term insurance the costlier permanent insurance to be "self-insured" someday and no longer need the insurance. Before I address the "buy term and invest the rest" response, I would like to address the first two solutions.

If you say your spouse will remarry, have you ever had that conversation with your spouse before it became your conclusion? If not, I would suggest you do. If your spouse remarried, what would you want for them? Would you like the second marriage to be for love or for money? It is a lot easier when financial concerns can be removed from the remarriage question and the answer can come from the heart and not from the head. I would want my spouse's remarriage to reflect the same sentiment in which we were married—for love!

Lesson #1: What I was taught to be true about life insurance that has turned out not to be true, is that I did not need much life insurance because my spouse can always remarry. It is not true because if my spouse desires to remarry after my death, I want it to be out of love, not because of the need for money.

If you say your spouse can get a job, have you ever considered why your spouse is not working now, or has only one job? If it is for the consideration of child-rearing, does your dream of one of you staying home with children, change just because the income earner has died? During the period of dating and engagement, many dreams are constructed. After marriage, these dreams begin and are carried out over a lifetime. Life insurance is the only thing that can ensure that the dreams of our early years really do come true. Life insurance is not really a necessary evil—life insurance is a dream realizer. The necessary evil is paying for it. Traditional thinking says to, "buy term and invest the rest", it is the best option for the least cost.

Lesson #2: What I was taught to be true about not needing life insurance that has turned out not to be true, is that if my spouse must face the future without me (or my income), I do not want it to have to change all of the hopes and dreams we had together. I do not want her to have to work if she does not want to. I still want my children to go to the college of their choice. I do not want them to settle for something more affordable that does not offer the curriculum that they would like to pursue, or not attain a college degree at all.

Before we can calculate the cost of life insurance, we need to first calculate how much death benefit is necessary. Consider a wage earner earning $100,000 a year. This is a good amount to consider, because it is easily scalable; if you earn $200,000, just double the calculations, and so on. If a spouse needed to replace $100,000 per year, and they could earn 5% consistently and safely, a nest egg of $2,000,000 would be necessary. Some would consider this nest egg the deceased's human life value, but it falls short when you account for what the future may hold. All this amount means is that the family could continue to live at the same standard of living without the need to generate the lost wage through trading their time for money. That is twenty times income, and for many insurance companies, it stretches the upper limits of what they will provide. This ignores the likelihood of earning 5% every year without fail and the family's need for periodic lump sums for things like cars, vacations, college educations, and weddings. Add these to the mix, and the answer to the deceased person's human life value is better defined by getting as much life insurance as the insurance company is willing to provide.

Lesson #3: What I was taught to be true about "buy term and invest the rest" that has turned out not to be true, is there is no sum of money that an insurance company will issue that can fund the hopes and desires that my family and I dreamed about.

Term life insurance can be purchased in various ways, either with an annual premium that increases with age, or a premium that stays level for a certain period of time and then increases with age. At a certain point, the annual increases in cost are prohibitive, but that is designed to happen after the children are grown, through college, and on their own. It is now that Mom and Dad in their retirement years no longer feel the "need" for life insurance; therefore, when it gets too expensive, they just drop the policy and consider themselves "self-insured." They become "self-insured" because during that same time period, they accumulate a nest egg equal to the amount of term life insurance that just expired. These two premises are the hallmarks of the "buy term and invest the rest" rule.

Let us consider a hypothetical 25-year-old, just married and starting a family, earning $100,000 per year. The hypothetical premium for a $2,000,000 life insurance contract whose premium is level for ten years, with the buyer in the best of health, and with no bells and whistles for "convertibility" or "premium waivers for disability," is $385 per year for ten years. Pretty cheap!

Let us stop right there, because I was taught that when purchasing life insurance, you should pay as little as possible; do not purchase all those extra riders. However, there is value in these riders you will want to consider before you dismiss them.

The rider for "convertibility" is a provision that allows you to convert your term policy death benefit, within a specified period of time, to a permanent life insurance policy. Conversion comes with the benefit of not having to have your health rescreened for pricing and issuance purposes. If you are buying term and investing the difference, why would you ever consider anything other than another term policy?

Consider a few scenarios.

Scenario 1: You are at the end of the level portion of your term policy. The $385 is about to go up to $4,445 in year eleven, and during the last ten years you have started to smoke. Your alternative here is to take another term policy, but no longer at the best insurance rates. Once the insurance company realizes you picked up the habit of smoking during the last ten years, the new ten-year term policy is no longer $385 a year but is now $4,085. This is still not $4,445, but it is a lot of money. You choose this new policy, but now you do not have much of the "invest the rest" money left, and the plan fails. In another ten years, you have the same decision to make, and to continue this new term policy will now cost $18,365!

Scenario 2: Your life has gone according to plan; however, toward the conclusion of your last term policy at age sixty-four, you are diagnosed with terminal cancer, and you are not expected to live more than another five years. You could keep the original plan in place and surrender the term policy, but after coming to terms with your shortened life expectancy, you realize that there is now a significant investment opportunity for your family. The soon to pay death benefit offers a better rate of return than you ever experienced in your "invest the rest" approach, by keeping your term policy. If you keep this last term policy, having paid $5,985 per year for each of the last ten years, the cost to continue the policy in year eleven is $61,965, but for a redemption value of $2,000,000 (a 3,000% rate of return), it is a now a fantastic investment. If you live past the eleventh year, the twelfth-year premium is $68,125: still a two-year rate of return of 1,400%. If you live twice the number of years your doctor first estimated (ten more years), your rate of return will still average more than 10% per year. The return might be great, but the problem it presents is complex.

- Each year you must mentally reconsider your diagnosis and your mortality, even though you are "beating it."
- You will need to pump over $970,000 into the term life insurance policy, and you might live longer than another ten years.

- If, at any point after paying that eleventh-year premium, you stop funding the life insurance policy, it makes the previous year's decision to pay the premium a poor decision.
- As you pay the premiums each year, and you live off your "invest the rest" nest egg, what is the status of your nest egg?
- If the original term policy had the term-to-permanent insurance conversion rider, the smoking decision and the cancer diagnosis would not have been an issue. The rider would have provided alternatives that are now not available because this rider was not purchased with the original term insurance policy.

Lesson #4: What I was taught to be true about "buy term and invest the rest" that has turned out not to be true, is that there is both economic and emotional value in the convertibility rider of a life insurance policy. The economic value comes from being able to keep the same level of death benefit for a set future cost, despite health changes. The emotional value comes from not having to revisit my mortality each year, should I ever have to "beat" a disease. The consideration of paying another enormous premium each year alone could be hazardous to my health.

The other rider that I was taught to avoid when buying term and investing the rest, was the rider that would waive the premium for the life insurance, should I ever become disabled. Studies by the Social Security Administration demonstrate that a twenty-year-old worker has a 30% chance of becoming disabled before they reach retirement age. (Source: www.ltdrates.com.) A 40-year-old male is twice as likely to become disabled before age 65 than he is to die. (Source: http://www.protectyourincome.com/education-center/disabilityfacts-and-statistics/probability.) Given the previous example regarding the convertibility lesson, for that same person who was diagnosed with cancer, the disability waiver would eliminate the continual "investment" of future premiums until the eventual $2,000,000 payoff at death. Now that is a rate of return, we cannot even calculate!

Lesson #5: What I was taught to be true about "buy term and invest the rest" that has turned out not to be true, is there is also economic and emotional value in the disability waiver of a premium rider of a life insurance policy. The economic value comes from not having to make continual premium payments during years of lower income because of disability. The emotional value is having the peace of mind that when the eventual death occurs, the hopes and dreams of a family will still live on without the additional monetary outlays.

Back to the hallmark of "buy term and invest the rest", buy enough temporary "death" insurance to replace the wage earner's income, then, invest what you would have otherwise spent on permanent life insurance to reach the status of being "self-insured".

Remember, the suggested minimum insurance for a 25-year-old, earning $100,000 a year is $2,000,000. That amount of temporary term insurance costs $385 per year for the first ten years.

At this individual's age 35, the premium on this policy goes to $4,445, not very cheap anymore, so they go shopping for another ten-year level-term policy. This time, their health has slipped a bit, a little cholesterol problem. The premium for their new $2,000,000 policy becomes $585, which is still considered inexpensive. But they begin to have a problem. The $585 no longer covers their human life value, because in those ten years between ages 25 and 35, they have received compensation increases and is now earning $150,000. Now their human life value is $3,000,000, and the premium goes to $835. If you are thinking, "they don't really need that much," stop and consider what you would be willing to cut out of your family (age 35) lifestyle. Your family may now include not only your spouse, but also children, ages eight, five, and two.

In ten years, you face the same decision. You are now 45 years of age; you have one child entering college and two in high school. Your income is now $200,000, and your term premium in year eleven is $14,065. You decide to apply for another ten-year policy. The insurance company may now start to lower its multiple on you. Instead of providing twenty times your income, the company may provide only fifteen times your income; after all, you were supposed to be "investing the rest." If the company will provide the same $3,000,000 at one more reduced health rating, because you have become "too short" for the same health rating. That means that your height has not kept up with your weight changes. Your new ten-year premium would be $2,875 per year. Now, it is not an affordable increase as it was ten years ago. A big decision looms, your cost just went from $835 to $2,875, with your oldest child just entering college and two not far behind!

Now you are 55, and you figure you must work to 65 because you must replace all that tuition you spent from the "invest the rest" pile. You realize a very subtle cost of "buy term and invest the rest" that no one told you about. Because you have been so successful in this approach, your asset level is determined by the government to be enough to pay for college. You are told your children do not qualify for higher education financial aid. Your "family contribution" eliminates the availability for aid.

At 55 you now have one more ten-year time frame to cover. Reducing the multiplier to ten times your income, assuming you have topped off at $200,000 per year, your last ten-year policy is at standard rates, since there is now some negative family history to your personal health record, and you find yourself spending $6,255 per year.

You make all the necessary sacrifices along the way and it is now the night before your official retirement dinner, and you are alone with your spouse at your favorite restaurant. You look lovingly into your spouse's eyes, and you begin to reminisce about all those years of working and raising a family. You tell your spouse that the plan has worked, that all those years of paying for all that cheap term insurance has finally come to an end. Tomorrow you are going to cancel your policy. Today, your spouse would get $2,000,000, but tomorrow, because your plan was so successful, they will get $0. Hope you make it through the night!

Let us add up all that cheap insurance. The $385 per year for the first ten years is $3,850. The second ten-year premium of $835 per year $8,350. The third ten-year premium of $2,875 per year is $28,750, and $6,255 for each of the last ten years is $62,550, for a grand total of $103,500. But that is only part of the cost. What you are not counting is what you otherwise could have earned on that money had you not spent it. Remember, the miracle of compound interest is stunted whenever you spend it. This is known as opportunity cost. Every dollar spent is a dollar that can never be saved or spent again, and neither can it earn what it might have earned while in your possession. If we put the flows of money for what the term insurance cost over those 40 years in an account earning 6% (your "invest the rest" experience), you discover that the true cost of that insurance was $227,638. Your next realization is that these funds will not be refunded to you, even though the life insurance company never had to pay out the death benefit. These funds are not going to be available for your use in retirement.

Assuming you live to life expectancy, another 20 years, that amount of money the life insurance company did not refund continued to grow for the life insurance company at 6%. Your $227,638 has now become $730,067; surely that will be refunded to your children now that you have passed on. No, in fact, the insurance company continues to keep it, and keeps it another 20 years, to the point at which you would have been 100 years of age. The insurance company has the tidy sum of $1,749,649, an amount of money that almost equals your initial death benefit when you were 25 years old, and an amount of money that certainly would have served both you and your children well in all your retirement years. All of this assumes that you succeeded at your "buy term and invest the rest" objective, you did not die before retirement.

Lesson #6: What I was taught to be true about "buy term insurance and invest the rest" that has turned out not to be true, is that term insurance is not the least expensive way to buy life insurance. It is an awfully expensive way to buy life insurance, when all the costs are accounted for.

Human nature plays a role in this age-old approach. The complement to "buy term" is "invest the rest." If you do not invest the rest, this plan does not work; in fact, it fails miserably! All the other factors noted in previous chapters come into play here, and usually somewhere along the way, "invest the rest" is abandoned. Whatever was intended to be invested is spent for things like vacation and college educations. The reality of "invest the rest" is that it does not happen.

Lesson #7: What I was taught to be true about "buy term insurance and invest the rest" that has turned out not to be true, is that few people invest the rest.

As shown in the "Rate of Return" and "Be a Long-Term Investor" chapters, the rates of return advertised in the marketplace just are not what the individual investor realizes. Remember that in the last 20 years, the 20 year "average" was 7.68% each year. However, factoring in how your money actually grew in the S&P 500, your "actual" annual rate of return was 6.06%. These rates include the strongest bull market in the history of the stock market, 2009-2019. When you factor in the Covid-19 virus inspired correction through March 22, 2020, the "average" falls to 5.96% and the "actual" rate of return falls to 4.3%.

Remember, because your actual experience in the market is year-to-year, not only do you earn something less than the average that is advertised, but you must also pay investment fees and income taxes on the growth. If you did your investing in your employer 401(k) or 403(b) plan or personal traditional IRA, the taxes you owe will apply on the entire account balance, at whatever the tax rate is at the time you begin to withdraw the money from the account.

If you pursued the permanent life insurance approach, your policy may have been designed with the intention of distributing funds from the life insurance contract prior to your death. The eventual withdrawals from your permanent life insurance contract, if withdrawn properly, with the expert help of your life insurance agent, will come to you without a tax. In fact, it will be sent to you in a way that is not even reportable to the Internal Revenue Service by either you or your life insurance company.

The benefits of proper withdrawals from a life insurance contract have a snowball effect. Because these distributions are not reportable on your tax return, they are not considered when determining whether your social security payments are taxable. If your only additional income in retirement is from your permanent life insurance contract, your social security may also be tax-free. If, instead, your additional cash flow in retirement comes from a qualified plan such as a 401(k), 403(b), or IRA, or even tax-free municipal bonds, that cash flow is accounted for when determining the taxability of your social security payments. This could result in up to 85% of your social security payments being subject to income tax at whatever the tax rate is that year.

Lesson #8: What I was taught to be true about "buy term insurance and invest the rest" that has turned out not to be true, is that, as evidenced by the last twenty years, it is exceedingly difficult to beat the capital equivalent value rate of return of a permanent life insurance contract after the fees and taxes are accounted for.

The Capital Equivalent Value rate of return is developed and explained more fully in <u>Confessions of a CPA: The Capital Equivalent Value of Life Insurance.</u>

BRYAN S. BLOOM

8

Permanent Life Insurance

"Society is always taken by surprise at any new example of common sense."
Ralph Waldo Emerson

"It is common sense to take a method and try it. If it fails, admit it frankly and try another."
Franklin D. Roosevelt

Many of the people I know with large amounts of cash-value permanent life insurance on themselves and on key family members, do not know how to use it. There will be many times in your business or your personal life that you will need access to cash or capital. Prematurely accessing your life insurance can serve that purpose. The cash value of your life insurance will become your "private reserve" that will be available for you to collateralize to access your death benefits. You can use this reserve for major purchases such as a car, tuition, wedding expenses or unexpected business needs. It is available to use as an emergency fund, or just to build a retirement fund that is available, exempt from income taxes. As your cash value grows, you are building up your "collateral capacity". This will allow you to forgo traditional secured bank financing and set up your own unstructured loan from the life insurance company. You use your cash value as collateral for the loan. Outstanding loans and unpaid interest on these loans directly reduce the amount of death benefits paid at your death.

When we talk about this kind of life insurance, we are not talking about just any kind of permanent life insurance. We are talking about custom-designed, cash-value permanent life insurance, funded up to but not over the government allowable modified endowment contract (MEC) limits. This will focus the policy on the available cash, but more importantly the leverage opportunities of that cash as collateral capacity.

The reason these MEC limits are so important is that the MEC limit is what defines the account as life insurance according to the IRS. Loans from permanent life insurance policies are tax exempt. Loans and withdrawals from a modified endowment contract may be subject to tax. If that distribution is prior to age 59 1/2, a 10% federal tax penalty may apply.

A qualified adviser will show you how to structure the life insurance policy properly, and once you have the money in the policy, it will become the lifeblood of your financial portfolio. It will eliminate the need for many of the other money buckets you were told in the past you needed. This one bucket will do the work of several, and it will give you liquidity, use, and control of your money.

Lesson #1: What I was taught to be true about life insurance that has turned out not to be true, is that life insurance is about more than just its value at death.

Another advantage of permanent life insurance is that it allows you higher contribution limits than you might have with qualified plan funds, while still maintaining tax-deferred growth.

Lesson #2: What I was taught to be true about life insurance that has turned out not to be true, is that life insurance is not a commodity; it is a unique tool, and when structured properly, can be one of the most valuable assets you can own.

Once this pool of money is properly established and structured, it will never drop in value and will continue to grow uninterrupted during a recession or even a depression. The money can be used for any expense you incur, or for any opportunity that you may find.

Lesson #3: What I was taught to be true about life insurance that has turned out not to be true, is that life insurance, during my lifetime, may be more about the "living benefits" and not only about the death benefits. I was never taught about the "living benefits"; I was always taught I had to die.

You may think that life insurance as I have described is complicated, but it is not. Let me explain with a story.

Remember back when you were eight years old and started your first paper route? You only made about $22 per month, so it took quite some time to save any money. Your goal may have been to eventually save $100 so you could buy that incredible ten-speed, metallic-blue bike. You would go and look at that bike in the bicycle shop each week. It probably took about six months' pay to finally have enough in your savings to purchase the bike. What a great day it was going to be. You may still remember it as if it were yesterday. The day finally arrived, and you walked down to the bank and asked the teller to give you all the money in your account. The teller gave you the $100, you put it in your pocket, and went straight to the bike shop. It was absolutely one of the best days of your life, and the bike was worth every penny of that $100!

The reason I tell this story is that on the surface, everything worked out, and you got good use out of your money. This was your vehicle of choice for the next few years while delivering papers, getting to school, having fun with friends, and so on. But if we look a little closer, we will realize that you no longer had any money in your savings account. Just as you were starting to see your interest begin to grow, you were back to zero. You would have to work for several more months just to get back to where you were when you purchased the bicycle.

For everything we buy we make two decisions. First, how to make the purchase and the second, how to pay for the purchase. We think that if we pay cash, it is only one decision, what to buy and we only have the second decision if we finance a purchase when we do not have the cash. However, when we pay cash, the cash we pay is no longer in the account where it was earning interest or dividends. In fact, we are borrowing not from the bank, but from our own future. The lost earnings represent the financing cost of the transaction.

Imagine if that $100 were still in your account and growing with interest while you had the use of the bike. At a 5% interest rate, that $100 would have grown to $776 by age 50. If my money is in a permanent life insurance contract, once the cash value in my policy is established, I would have the collateral capacity to structure my purchase in a way that benefits me the most. This simple bicycle illustration can be expanded to anything you purchase, and you can apply this same principle to your full advantage.

Lesson #4: What I was taught to be true about life insurance that has turned out not to be true, is that a permanent life insurance contract is not just a one-dimensional financial product. The cash value within a permanent life insurance contract will grow and build collateral capacity, so that other compounding interest accounts will not be diminished every time you make a purchase.

If you have a permanent life insurance policy equal to the value of your retirement assets, you will be able to consume your other assets in retirement, not merely live on what interest they can pay. You can spend freely because you know that the value of your death benefits will someday replenish all the money you spent during retirement.

Lesson #5: What I was taught to be true about life insurance that has turned out not to be true, is that I was taught you do not really need life insurance past retirement age. However, at retirement your permanent life insurance contract may unlock the true value of your other assets, as they are consumed to sustain your retirement lifestyle.

If anyone tells you that you do not need life insurance, ask them if they will provide the money your spouse and children will need to pay the bills that do not go away at your untimely death.
Permanent life insurance is the only way to assure that what you want to happen will happen. It takes the guesswork out of saving for the future, and it takes away the uncertainty that you may have when all your money tied up in risk-based investments.

What being "self-insured" will do for you is to put you back into a situation of spending your compounding interest accounts, just as you may have done to purchase your first bicycle, stunting your true potential.

However, just as with any financial asset, permanent life insurance can be abused if not used properly.

If excessive tax-free loans are taken and the policy lapses, a taxable event could occur. Consult with a qualified adviser to be sure that your life insurance contract is set up properly. Your goal should be to get the full benefit of a permanent life insurance policy. This includes avoiding taxes, fees and penalties that come with other investments, without any unintended negative consequences.

Lesson #6: What I was taught to be true about life insurance that has turned out to be true, is that it can be abused if not utilized properly, resulting in negative consequences.

If you pursue a permanent life insurance strategy, you must have a good road map and co-pilot. I doubt you would head out from New York, with Los Angeles as your destination, and not have a road map by your side or at least your navigation system activated. Do not try to do this alone, find an advisor who is skilled in the proper use and care of permanent life insurance.

BRYAN S. BLOOM

9

Your Home Is Your Greatest Asset

"Common sense will nearly always stand you in better stead than a slavish adherence to the conventions."
M.M. Kaye

"It has been said that there is nothing more uncommon than common sense."
Thomas Chalmers

Even after the real estate bubble burst in 2008, people still consider their homes to be their greatest asset.

During the thirty years prior to the decline in home prices, home prices consistently increased year after year. That growth happened regardless of what the homeowner did or did not do, as long as they performed routine maintenance of the property. Because the homeowner lived in the house, they did not face the decision of whether to stay in the market or get out. In fact, unless forced to sell, because of other unwise financial decisions, today's homeowner continues to "stay in the market". This is because the house represents their home, rather than an investment. The homeowner does not experience the stress of watching their values go down during a down cycle, thinking there is a better alternative elsewhere. Recognizing the house as your home rather than as an investment, is the proper viewpoint, rather than seeing your home as the greatest asset. Your home is a place to make memories, not money.

We will look at an example to illustrate a few points.

Purchase price	$200,000
Purchase date	January 1995
Market price (2007) prior to the bubble bursting	$380,000

Had this homeowner cashed out of the property in 2007, the total rate of return for the thirteen-year period would have been 72%. This appears to be a great return. However, when broken down, as we break down other investment returns, to an average annual rate of return, that would have been 4.3% per year. A bit more modest in how our brain interprets this gain. However, the homeowner is focused on neither the 72% nor the 4.3%, but instead on the increase of $160,000.

Lesson #1: What I was taught to be true about my home being my best investment that has turned out not to be true, is that I was taught to focus on the wrong number.

There is nothing wrong with a gain of $160,000, or even 4.3% per year, especially when I consider that under current tax law, that gain is income tax free. It rivals many investments available today.

But that is not the whole story. Suppose let us assume the homeowner had properly insured his home for a loss that might have been experienced through a fire, tornado, flood, earthquake, hurricane, or other peril. In the Midwest (without the threat of a hurricane), the typical cost of a homeowner's insurance policy for our example would cost conservatively $1,500 per year.

To properly account for the gain or return on an investment, all costs associated with holding the investment must be accounted for.

This required "holding" cost of your home, when the house is considered an asset, reduces the monetary gain from $160,000 to $140,500. Consequently, this brings the average rate of return down from 4.3% to 3.9%. This a required holding cost. If you own your home with a mortgage associated with it, the mortgage company is going to require you to obtain a homeowner's insurance contract. If you fail to insure the property, your mortgage company will, at an enormous rate! One of the pieces of paper, in the stack of forms you signed at your home closing, was an agreement that allows your mortgage company to buy insurance if you fail to do so. If you happen to own your home outright, not owning casualty insurance for it is plain foolish.

Homeowner's insurance is not the only required holding cost. One of the ways we finance our local government and their services, is through a tax on real estate. The amount of real estate tax varies from state to state. The real estate tax for the Illinois home example would have averaged around $8,000 per year. In thirteen years, this homeowner would have paid $104,000 in real estate taxes. Factoring this in as a holding cost, drives the monetary gain down to $36,500 and the annual rate of return down to 1.2%.

In addition to the holding costs, there are maintenance costs. These are voluntary, but if you do not do them, your home appreciation will not be as described. This home was purchased when it was seven years old, so in 2007, it was a twenty-year-old home. During the course of ownership, this homeowner did the following:

Update the Landscaping	$3,000
Repaired the Property Grading and Drainage	$5,000
Replaced the Roof	$10,000
Upgraded the Interior Decorating	$5,000
Replaced Half of the Windows	$3,500
Replaced the Air Conditioning and Furnace	$5,000
TOTAL	$31,500

Accounting for these necessary maintenance costs, the annual rate of return becomes .2%. Not exactly the rate of return we expect from our "greatest asset."

These costs are quite modest. Spend a bit more, and you might have lost money on this piece of property!

Lesson #2: What I was taught to be true about my home being my best investment that has turned out not to be true, is when I account for all the costs associated with keeping the asset, the rate of return on the overall value of the house decreases dramatically.

Now let us consider the market for real estate. In 2011, this same home had a market value of $265,000, no longer $380,000. Now, the annual rate of return over seventeen years is a negative 3%, even though it is still worth $45,000 more than what you paid for it — certainly not your greatest financial asset.

Lesson #3: What I was taught to be true about my home being my best investment that has turned out not to be true, is that I was taught my home was a virtually riskless asset.

Associated with home ownership is home ownership financing. Home ownership financing is where the "greatest asset" term ought to be applied. However, we are taught that debt is bad and that we ought to avoid debt and get the home paid off as soon as possible.

What is the least expensive way to purchase a home? Is it with cash? Is it with a 15-year mortgage? or with a 30-year mortgage? Let us simplify the math and this time use a home purchased for $250,000. We also need to consider what the investor's best alternative rate of return might be. Let us assume the best the investor can do in the investment markets is 5%. We also need to consider the tax savings of mortgage deductibility; with a marginal tax rate of 30% for both federal and state income taxes combined.

Most would assume that the least costly way to purchase the home, if you had the money, would be to pay cash. That would be an outlay of $250,000. If the purchaser pays $250,000, that means he or she does not have $250,000 to invest any longer. Since we are going to compare this to a 15 and a 30-year mortgage, we need to pick the evaluation period as the longest period, thirty years. In thirty years, invested at 5%, the $250,000 would grow to $1,080,485. So, the cost to live in the home over thirty years, if the purchaser pays cash, is $1,080,485.

Comparing the two mortgages, assume the following:

| Down Payment of 20% | $50,000 |
| Amount Borrowed | $200,000 |

	30 Year Mortgage	15 Year Mortgage
Interest Rate	6%	5.5%
Investment Rate of Return	5%	5%
Interest Expended	$231,676	$94,150

*The lower the interest rate paid, the greater discrepancy between the 15 and 30-year mortgage. It would have been too easy to assume the home mortgage rates of 2021 (less than 3%) for this comparison. If it is much easier to earn more than 3% than it is 5%. The emphasis of this section is to show that even when the investment rate is less than the interest cost, paying cash is still the most expensive way to purchase your home.

Many people stop the analysis right there and conclude that they do not want to spend as much in interest as the home costs. Therefore, based only on interest paid, they decide to pay cash. If they do not have the cash, they decide that the 15-year mortgage is better than the 30-year mortgage because they will pay $137,526 less in interest.

However, just as with home appreciation, that is not the whole story. Every year, they pay mortgage interest. Because mortgage interest is potentially a tax-deductible item, you must include the tax savings that they will experience. Furthermore, the tax savings need to be brought forward to the 30-year evaluation horizon at the assumed investment rate of 5%. When you do that, the chart looks like this:

An interesting fact shows up here. In this example, the tax savings invested for the 30-year time frame more than offsets the actual interest expended on the 15-year loan. In other words, over thirty years, the interest expended is recaptured via tax savings and returned to your wealth potential. Recaptured is an important word. In every financial decision, it is economically advisable to recoup as many costs as possible, as you accumulate wealth.

Looking at net interest only, you would now favor the 15-year mortgage over the outlay of cash, even if you had the cash. In fifteen years, you would have completely covered the interest cost by the tax savings invested. But that is still not the entire story.

To get to an honest bottom line, you must carry all the calculations out for the entire thirty years. Not just the interest expended, or the taxes saved, but also the outlays of monthly principal payments that are part of your monthly mortgage payments.

Notice that I have eliminated a couple of lines in the chart below:

1. I have replaced the interest expended with interest otherwise invested. I have done this because merely paying interest is not what is important. What is important is what you would have otherwise done with the money if you had not had a mortgage payment.
2. I have also eliminated the tax savings and more accurately accounted for the tax savings invested, as described above.
3. I have added an "all cash" column and identified the "all cash" as a down payment. After all, isn't that what it is?
4. I have added a line to account for the principal payments made each year on your mortgage and assumed that you would have been able to invest that at 5% if you did not own the home.

	All Cash	30 Year Mortgage	15 Year Mortgage
Interest Rate		6%	5.5%
Investment Rate of Return	5%	5%	5%
Interest Otherwise Invested		$626,480	$326,765
Tax Savings Invested		$187,944	$98,029
Down Payment Invested	$1,080,485	$216,097	$216,097
Monthly Payment Invested		$371,482	$596,489
Net Cost to Own Home	$1,080,485	$1,026,115	$1,041,322

The bottom line in this example is that the most expensive way to purchase your home is with all cash; the best way to buy it is with a 30-year mortgage. The difference is over $54,000, just in the way you purchase your home.

Do not be deceived by the lack of mortgage interest tax deductibility. The 2021 standard deduction on our joint tax returns is over $25,000. Many people no longer itemize their deductions, effectively removing the advantage of getting a tax advantage for paying interest. However, economic times change, and our government has many levers to pull to stimulate one segment of the economy if they choose. Currently the housing market does not need stimulation. Someday it may, and one of the stimulus levers may be to restore the tax deductibility of mortgage interest for more taxpayers.

Also, I, purposely positioned the interest rates as close to each other as possible. Individual circumstances may cause the analysis to differ. However, the greater the spread between the mortgage rate and the reinvestment rate, and the closer the spread between the interest rates of a 15-year and a 30-year mortgage, the more dramatic the difference will be between your three choices, still favoring the 30-year mortgage.

Lesson #4: What I was taught to be true about my home being my best investment that has turned out not to be true, is that I was taught to pay off my mortgage as quickly as possible. However, just the opposite is true.

Another wealth concept to consider is inflation. Sometimes we dismiss this, because we think inflation is going to occur regardless of what we do. This is a reality that my future is going to need to absorb. There is nothing we can do about it. However, when it comes to paying your mortgage, there is something you can easily address. It can be simply summed up with this question. If you have a fixed dollar obligation, when would you rather pay that obligation? When your dollar is worth more or when it is worth less?

A simple example illustrates this point. Assume a mortgage obligation is $1,000 per month and you can pay an extra $1,000 toward your mortgage obligation. Would you rather send the bank $1,000 today that would otherwise purchase $1,000 worth of other goods and services or would you rather send $1,000 to the bank 30 years from now, when those dollars will only purchase $552 worth of goods and services? Do you want to spend $1,000 or $552?

Lesson #5: What I was taught to be true about my home being my best investment that has turned out not to be true, is that I was encouraged to pay off my home loan as fast as possible. Now I know I would rather pay the mortgage with deflated future dollars, rather than today's expensive dollars.

The real opportunity, if you value pursuing the "best rate of return" perspective, comes from having as little of your own money as possible tied up in your home. This is because the rate of return on the equity in your home is 0%.

Consider two identical homes, one across the street from the other. They are both valued at $200,000. One is purchased with the minimum down payment of $40,000 (20%), and the other is purchased with a down payment of $100,000.

If the market value of each home increases by $10,000, each home is now worth $210,000. If the homes are sold, who gets the extra $10,000? Choose from the following possible answers.

1. All the gain goes to the bank, since without its money you would not have been able to own the home.
2. The money is shared with the mortgage lender since it owns part of the home. In this situation, the homeowner of House 1 would receive $2,000 of the increase, and the homeowner of House 2 would receive $5,000. Each increase representing the percentage of the homeowner's ownership.
3. Each of the homeowners will get all the money.

Since the answer is (c), each of the homeowners, the amount of equity in the home is extraneous information. Therefore, the rate of return on home equity is 0%. It does not matter how much equity is ascribed to the homeowner.

I was always taught to calculate my rate of return on every investment. Even though I know my return on equity is 0%, let us do what we are taught, just to illustrate a point. In the gain of $10,000 on the $200,000 houses, remember that it did not matter how much equity you had in the house; all the gain was the homeowners. But, if you really want to calculate a rate of return, a $10,000 gain on a $100,000 investment is 10%, and a $10,000 gain on a $40,000 investment it is 25%. But remember, if you could have purchased the home with no down payment, a $10,000 gain on a $0 investment is an infinite rate of return. You cannot get better than that! If you really want a rate of return to make you feel better, which would you rather have, 10%, 25%, or an infinite rate of return?

Lesson #6: What I was taught to be true about my home being my best investment that has turned out not to be true, is that I was taught equity in my home has a positive rate of return. Again, just the opposite is true. There is no investment value in an equity position of a home. The appreciation of the home's value is not dependent on your equity investment. Either the house appreciates, or it does not. If it appreciates, all the gain belongs to the homeowner, without regard to the amount of equity they have in the house.

In fact, one can argue that the larger your equity position, the more at risk you are.

Again, consider the two identical $200,000 homes. Not only are the two homes identical, but the family structures in each home are identical as well. Happily married couples with two grade school children. Both wives are radio personalities for the local radio station, and both husbands are top-notch reporters for the local newspaper. Their incomes are identical, and each income is necessary to pay the bills each month, including the mortgages.

The first couple, Mr. and Ms. Huge Debt, owes $160,000 on their home (they made the minimum down payment), and the second couple, Mr. and Ms. Max Down, owes $100,000 (they made a $100,000 down payment).

Assume further that both couples just inherited $90,000. What should they do with the money?

Believing in the logic of establishing as much equity in your home as possible, the Down's take the $90,000 to their mortgage lender and pay the mortgage down to $10,000. Their belief of having as much equity in their home as possible, they have bought in so strongly that they have no other savings, other than in their "greatest asset." However, the Debt's decide to buy a certificate of deposit at their local bank.

What happened to the Down's mortgage payment? Was it reduced to reflect their $90,000 pre-payment? No, it remains the same; they will just pay off the mortgage that much faster, which falls right into their plans.

If Max suffers a career-ending disability, what happens to the Down's ability to pay their mortgage? It suffers a big blow. Will the mortgage lender take into consideration that just a month before they brought in a check for $90,000 and applied it to their outstanding debt? No! Will the mortgage lender take into consideration that they have been paying their mortgage on the lender's biweekly plan and are ahead on their mortgage by four months? No! What does the bank care about? It cares about the next month's mortgage payment being paid in full.

What happens when the mortgage check does not arrive? The Down's are assessed a late penalty, and their credit report takes a hit. What about when they cannot make the payment in the second month of Max's disability? Same thing. What about the third month? A foreclosure sign goes up in the front yard!

What if Max had never prepaid the mortgage when they received the inheritance? He would have the $90,000 in the bank to draw down monthly, if necessary, to make the mortgage payment. That is 7 ½ years if the mortgage payment is $1,000 per month. No bad credit reports and no foreclosure sign.

Lesson #7 What I was taught to be true about my home being my best investment that has turned out not to be true, is that it is always more efficient to have the ability to pay off the mortgage with a safe side fund, just in case you cannot from your income.

What happens if, instead of a disability, there is a downturn in the economy, and the radio station uses all nationally syndicated shows and eliminates the local talent? As a result, the economic downturn results in a housing value decline of 25%. Now each home is worth only $150,000. Who is in the safer position? Huge Debt is upside down in his mortgage. He owes $160,000 on a home worth $150,000. It looks bad. Max Down feels rather good; he owes just $10,000, even though his home has fallen in value.

However, the Down's are in trouble if they cannot make the mortgage payment. Again, it is three strikes, and they are out, and the lender feels rather good about collecting the $10,000 mortgage balance from a home worth $150,000.

The Debt's are a bit nervous. For them it is three strikes, and they are out as well, but the bank is a bit reluctant to satisfy the $160,000 debt with the sale of the $150,000 house. Instead of foreclosing on the Debt's house, the lender agrees to waive the early withdrawal penalty on the $90,000 Certificate of Deposit so that the Debt's can continue to pay their mortgage.

Lesson #8 What I was taught to be true about my home being my best investment that has turned out not to be true, is that the lower your mortgage balance, the more at risk you are of losing your down payment or any other equity you have in the house, and the lender is safer.

How wrong is the statement, "your home is your most valuable asset"? Consider the following:

The 30-year mortgage payment of $1,200 per month in the above example would have purchased a $250,000 asset (the house) and would be worth $606,000 if the home appreciated in value by 3% each year without any holding or improvement costs.

What if a 35-year-old couple could invest the $1,200 per month in a simple permanent life insurance contract, considered by most to be a stable and consistently growing asset. By the time they were 65 and ready to retire, they could have $714,000 of cash value; equity they could spend in retirement. They would also have over $1,500,000 of death benefits. The death benefit could be left to their children as their inheritance, just as a paid off house would have. Which would they prefer? A $600,000 house or $1,500,000? The guarantees of an insurance policy are based on the claims-paying ability of the issuing insurance company.

Rather than cashing in the cash of the life insurance policy, those values could be leveraged to provide a tax-free retirement income of over $50,000 per year for the couple for 20 years in retirement. This would allow them to still leave over $400,000 of assets to the next generation. To generate this amount of retirement cash flow tax exempt in any other asset, that asset would have to earn almost 7% every year for 30 years, without fail, after taxes and after investment fees. This is the capital equivalent value of this life insurance policy assuming a 3.5% safe withdrawal rate. For more about capital equivalent value, please read <u>Confessions of a CPA, The Capital Equivalent Value of Life Insurance</u>. The third book in the series, Confessions of a CPA.

We start our lives chasing the American dream of owning our own home, our "most valuable asset." But when we understand the principles of this chapter, we find out that our "most valuable asset" is valuable not for the wealth it generates, but instead for the memories that develop as we raise our families. Houses were meant to be homes in which to raise families, not to store cash.

10

Asset Accumulation

"In the following pages I offer nothing more than
simple facts, plain arguments, and common sense;
and have no other preliminaries to settle with the reader,
than that he will divest himself of prejudice and repossession,
and suffer his reason and feelings to determine for themselves;
and that he will put on, or rather that he will not put off,
the true character of man,
and generously enlarge his view beyond the present day."
Thomas Paine

"Work hard, use your common sense and don't be afraid to trust
your instincts."
Fred L. Turner

It is said, "He who accumulates the most, wins the retirement race." Therefore, achieving the highest rate of return during your lifetime must be the goal. Can you spend a rate of return? No! You can only spend cold, hard cash. At the end of your life, as you look back, would you like to say you achieved the highest rate of return possible, or would you like to be able to say you enjoyed the highest standard of living your wealth could provide?

The goal of asset accumulation is like setting out to climb Mt. Everest without any plan to get back home. Is getting to the top the ultimate prize, or is it getting back down and tell others about it? If you die on the mountain, even after achieving the summit, were you successful?

Consider the following facts concerning the 29,035-foot peak of Mt. Everest. Between 1921 and 2006, 8,030 people set out to scale the mountain to the top. Only 28% achieved their goal and got to the top. That means 72% failed. Most of them quit before the summit and successfully got back to base camp to tell their story of failure. Almost 3% failed the climb miserably; not only did they not get to the summit, but neither did they get back down. They died on the mountain. The remains of 120 of them are still there. Of those who perished, 15% died on the way up; they never abandoned their climb, and they never came home to tell their stories. On the way down 73% died; they simply did not abandon their climb early enough to sustain the descent. Now, the most startling statistic of them all is that 56% of those who perished on the mountainside perished after having succeeded in getting to the top! They died on the way back to base camp, after achieving their goal.

Just as in mountain climbing, asset accumulation is only half of the story; asset distribution is as important, if not more important.

Lesson #1: What I was taught to be true about asset accumulation that has turned out not to be true, is that it is more important not to run out of money during our lifetimes than it is to accumulate the most.

There are two ways to distribute your retirement nest egg. In planning your retirement distribution plan, remember that retirement funds must last two lifetimes of a happily married couple.

The first and most conventional way to live out your retirement life is to take the approach of living on only what your invested assets earn. This is the interest only approach. That is all you budget to spend, interest or dividends only. You leave the principal alone; you do not touch it. During your working career, your effort is the engine that generates the income to support your lifestyle. In this retirement approach the principal of your assets is your income engine, and it must remain untouched.

In 2001 a certificate of deposit could have been purchased with a 5% guarantee for the length of the certificate maturity. This would lead you to the conclusion that you could live on the interest generated by the certificate of deposit. For instance, a $100,000 certificate of deposit would generate a $5,000 annual income.

However, by mid-2011, the five-year CD rate was 1.7% and falling every week (source: bankrate.com). If you renewed at this rate and were withdrawing 5% from your account, you would receive less and less each year to finance your retirement, not only because of the lower interest rate, but also because you have been spending down the principal to make up for the interest you were not earning. The only answer to the lower interest rates in the interest-only strategy is to reduce your standard of living, in this example by 66%. What would you plan on cutting back on? Travel? Medical expenditures? Entertainment? Gifts to the grandchildren?

Some of the obvious limits to the income only approach is the following:

- The accumulation of assets is especially important. At retirement, your assets must reach a certain level to generate an adequate amount of retirement income.
- Principal cannot be accessed deliberately for income.
- Fixed income for life provides no adjustment for inflation, resulting in a decrease of lifestyle every year.

The risks inherent to the interest-only approach are:

1. Inflation: Since you are living on only the interest that the nest egg provides; you have a fixed amount of income. Because inflation is eroding your purchasing power, you will likely experience a decrease in lifestyle.
2. Tax Rate: Since the government taxes the interest that you earn, you do not get to keep the entire amount of interest that is generated by the nest egg. What is the effect of the government raising the tax rates? You are still getting the same amount of income, but the government takes a larger share, so your spendable income is decreased.
3. Interest Rate: What happens to your income if the amount of interest you are earning decreases due to changes in the econ-

omy or the interest rate environment? Again, you experience a decrease in spendable income.

4. Loss of Capital: What happens if, either by choice or out of necessity, you need to spend your principal? Perhaps you have an unexpected medical expense, or you choose to help a child or grandchild with some money. Any amount of capital that you remove from your nest egg will affect the amount of interest that you will earn in the future, which will result in a decrease in spendable income.

5. Market Risk: To compensate for the first four risks, people choose to put a portion of their nest egg into the stock market, which introduces market risk to the equation.

Lesson #2: What I was taught to be true about asset accumulation that has turned out not to be true, is that there are major risks associated with living on just the growth my assets can provide.

The alternative approach is one in which you purposely consume some of your principal with the income strategy. The only reliable scenario for this approach is when there is a guaranteed life insurance death benefit equal to the beginning retirement asset balance for both spouses. The permanent death benefit returns the principal spent in retirement together to the surviving spouse. At this point in life, the life insurance is more about insuring your assets than your life. Without this safety net, you lack the "permission" to spend your principal. Do not choose the consume-principal approach to retirement income if you do not have this safety net. Guaranteed death benefits of a life insurance contract are dependent on the claims-paying ability of the issuing life insurance company.

This strategy is generally based on "average rates of return", "buy term and invest the rest," and "Monte Carlo" simulations. Some retirees choose to spend time at a casino as a retirement activity. Unfortunately, many set themselves up for such a casino lifestyle utilizing this approach of planning for retirement. They just do not know they are gambling with their financial lifestyle, with the investment markets and banking that averages are accurate.

A Monte Carlo simulation merely takes the market rates of return, mixes up the returns, and plays bingo with your money. Seems like a logical approach since bingo is another common retirement activity. The strategy looks at thousands of random sets of return scenarios to establish the likelihood that you will outlast your money. Along with the random sets of returns, you test various rates of distribution.

Even a 5% withdrawal rate has a high risk of your principal decreasing. The ten years between 1999 and 2008 is one example, because this was a period that would not have sustained a 5% withdrawal based on a 5% return assumption.

Remember this chart from the "Be a Long-Term Investor" chapter? Starting with a $100,000 nest egg, and withdrawing 5% each year we see the following:

This illustrates that during this ten-year period, thinking that the long-term average rate of return strategy of over 13% (60 history of the S&P 500 from 1939 – 1998), 5% should sustain you. At the end of ten years, your principal has been reduced by almost two-thirds! It just does not work if this ten-year period was during your distribution years.

Even after you add back the market recovery years of 2009 and 2010, it is still not pretty.

	Withdrawal	Rate of Return	Beginning of the Year	Gain or Loss	End of the Year
1999	5,000	19.51%	95,000	18,535	113,535
2000	5,000	-10.14%	108,535	(11,005)	97,529
2001	5,000	-13.04%	92,529	(12,066)	80,463
2002	5,000	-23.37%	75,463	(17,636)	57,828
2003	5,000	26.38%	52,828	13,936	66,763
2004	5,000	8.99%	61,763	5,553	67,316
2005	5,000	3.00%	62,316	1,869	64,185
2006	5,000	13.62%	59,185	8,061	67,247
2007	5,000	3.53%	62,247	2,197	64,444
2008	5,000	-38.49%	59,444	(22,880)	36,564
2009	5,000	23.49%	31,564	7,714	39,978
2010	5,000	12.78%	33,978	4,342	38,320

Look closely at 2010. Even a 12.78% gain is not enough to offset a 5% distribution based on the initial nest egg.

Lesson #3: What I was taught to be true about asset accumulation that has turned out not to be true, is that even if you are withdrawing a smaller average rate than what the long-term average rate is, you may withdraw more than you actually earn.

Beware of the difference between average and actual. As soon as you withdraw more dollars than you earn, the downslope gets very steep and is hard to recover. You cannot rectify this by simply applying the withdrawal rate to your actual annual balance. In this example, you could only withdraw $1,699 from your retirement nest egg in 2010, not $5,000. That is 66% less than what you were planning on. Average rates of return are not what you actually earn. In this example you either reduce your retirement lifestyle by 66% or you have 66% less money in your nest egg than you expected.

This is amazing; you would think that a 23% and a 12% return would have reestablished much of the wealth lost in 2008. A good thing to remember is that the percentage loss in the investment markets reduce your balance from a larger balance, making the actual dollar loss greater. Market gains increase your balance based on a smaller number, minimizing the dollar impact of a recovery.

The reason why many withdrawal strategies did not work in these twelve years is that the alternative to being invested in the stock market was to be invested in bonds or Certificates of Deposit at your local bank. Only five times during those twelve years were five-year CDs renewing at higher than 5%. If you had a CD that needed to be renewed in 2011, the renewal rate was less than 2%. That reality may have tempted you into adding risk to your retirement by entering the stock market with you nest egg. It has been getting worse every year since 2011. The interest rate in 2021 on a five-year CD was a whopping .85%.

The equity market returns since 2009 have certainly turned up. However, when you return your attention to the Be a Long-Term Investor chapter you will be reminded that since 2009, the market return has averaged almost 11% per year even though the actual return is just over 9%. Even in this extended bull market, 9% is a long way from the 13% posted between 1939 – 1998. When you consider the twenty year returns between 2000 and 2019, the actual return is just over 6%. Considering the first quarter correction of 2020 and the actual return is only 4.3% per year.

I have illustrated the time period of 1999 through 2008, a short period of time, because you need to prepare for the time when this 10-year period is your experience. The longer we live the shorter our time period is as well. There will be the day when we cannot plan on a 30-year average, when our life expectancy may be less than 10 years.

Lesson #4: What I was taught to be true about asset accumulation that has turned out not to be true, is that there is no such thing as being "self-insured" with a retirement nest egg. There is a need for permanent life insurance in retirement.

When life insurance is present during retirement, every asset is replenished at the first death, and the longer you live together in retirement, the shorter one member of the happily married couple will live as a survivor. The longer you live, you can even access the cash values for consumption, allowing you to retire earlier, enhancing your lifestyle, or reducing the pressure on your accumulation assets to perform.

The key features of the "consumption of principal and interest" strategy is the following:

- As you spend down your principal, you have more money to enjoy your retirement.
- The surviving spouse's income is covered with the deceased spouse's death benefit.
- Cash values of your life insurance policy provide you with less fear of running out of money.

Rather than having risks associated with this strategy, the risks associated with the income-only approach are mitigated.

1. Inflation: When you can consume your principal, you can mitigate inflation by increasing your distribution each year to keep up with inflation. The effect is that you can level your purchasing power.
2. Tax Rate: By spending some of your principal every year, you are reducing the size of your nest egg. This means there is less principal on which to earn interest in the succeeding years. As you earn less interest, you pay less tax. So, even if the tax rate increases in the future, there is less interest being earned, so it mitigates the impact of the tax increase.
3. Interest Rate: When you are consuming your own principal, a decrease in interest rate has less effect on your income than if you were trying to live on the interest alone.
4. Loss of Capital: You are already consuming your own capital, even though it would impact your spendable income, you would still have more spendable income than if you were trying to live on only the interest.
5. Market Risk: You could eliminate market risk with this alternative because you could construct a portfolio that would earn 2–3% without exposing any of the assets to the market. Because of your ability to consume your principal, you would still have more income than living off interest alone.

Lesson #5: What I was taught to be true about asset accumulation that has turned out not to be true, is that while I may not need life insurance, I would certainly want life insurance because of the protection of my assets in retirement, increases my spending flexibility.

Remember, the climb to the top is difficult and quite precarious, but the descent is fraught with even more obstacles, including those unseen and taken for granted as being safe. If something you thought to be true turned out not to be true, when would you want to know?

BRYAN S. BLOOM

11

Financing Large Purchases

"Everybody gets so much information all day long that they lose
their common sense."
Gertrude Stein

"The genius of a good leader is to leave behind him a situation
which common sense, without the grace of genius,
can deal with successfully."
Walter Lippmann

How you buy things may be the key to your secure financial future.

Every purchase, large or small, is a financing decision. As described in previous chapters, it is not just about interest charged on a purchase when you purchase with credit, but it is also about interest not earned if you use your own money.

What if you were the bank?

If you have any savings at all, you are the bank; you just do not know it. Because you do not know it, you do not treat yourself as a bank. If you treated yourself as a bank, you would pay yourself back for every purchase you made. Maybe, not every purchase, but certainly those that do not fit in your month-to-month budget. If you face an expenditure that cannot be covered by the current month's income, then, it must be covered by savings or a bank loan. If you cover it with savings, then you should replenish those savings from future month's income. Pay yourself back. A few examples of purchases and expenses of larger items are vehicles, college educations, homes, real estate taxes, and vacations. The list of pay yourself back purchases is personal and has infinite possibilities.

There are two keys to financial freedom, and both are related to your purchasing mentality.

1. Every time you make a purchase from your savings, pay yourself back.
2. Every time you have finished paying yourself or the bank back, keep paying yourself. Once a debt repayment is established, it becomes part of our monthly budget. Somehow, we figure

how the new monthly payment fits into the budget. When it is no longer a required monetary outlay, do not stop it; just change who you send the money to and save it.

Let us first consider traditional bank financing, more specifically financing a large purchase such as a car. When you purchase a car and you use traditional financing, you have the choice of using your bank or credit union or the convenience of the dealership's financing options. Timing is one of the problems with financing; you must first negotiate the purchase price of the car and then, generally at another location, negotiate the terms of your loan. Then bring the two together.

Many vehicle purchasers opt for the financing at the car dealership because it all can happen simultaneously. Another reason the bank is not even considered is because the interest rate at the dealership is so low. In many circumstances you can find 1.9% or 2.9% financing rates. Sometimes you can even find a 0% loan. That is like free money! This is a close cousin to the three year "same as cash" offers you find when you purchase other items. Frequently this is how furniture is sold. The only difference is that the "same as cash" requires no payments until just before the term is over, when it is due in full. Beware of being a day late with your payment. If you are late, all the interest that accrued during the three years would be payable.

The 0% from the car dealership is a bit different, it requires monthly payments.

The requirement of monthly payments is the first problem with the 0% loans. While the interest rate might be 0%, it still obligates you to a monthly payment that you might not be able to afford. I have worked with plenty of people who bought more car than they should have because the loan was "free."

Have you ever wondered why a car dealership can offer 0%? They can, because 0% is often not 0%, if you look at it carefully. Sometimes the 0% loan is the most profitable part of the new car purchase for the car dealership.

The small print of the 0% loan discloses that if you do not take advantage of the 0% loan, the dealership can offer you "cash back." An example would be the purchase of a $30,000 car at 0% or $4,000 cash back.

The payment associated with financing $30,000 at 0% for four years would be $625 per month for 48 months. It is easy math, just divide the purchase price by the number of months the payback is required. However, if you paid cash or borrowed the funds from a conventional bank, what is the real purchase price of the car? What is the amount of money you would need to give the car dealership when you take delivery of the car? The dealership would require the $30,000, less the $4,000 cash back. The real price of the car would be $26,000, not the $30,000 that is the basis of the 0% loan.

If you paid cash and financed yourself over the same time period at 0%, the payment to yourself would be $542 per month. Once again, simple math, the real purchase price, $26,000 divided by the number of months to complete the payback. For the same car, the car dealership is charging you over 15% more per month. This is because the car dealership is not really loaning the money. They typically must prepay the financing incentive to the actual lending institution the $4,000 they could have paid you as "cash back" so

CONFESSIONS OF A CPA

that they can offer the 0% loan. They build the financing incentive into a higher price for the car. Another way to think about it is that the "cash back" you do not get when you choose the 0% loan is simply prepaid interest.

Lesson #1: What I was taught to be true about large purchase financing that has turned out not to be true, is that 0% is not 0% when it costs me more money.

Once again, we are tricked by percentages, when we ought to be paying attention to our cash flows.

The next question is why do you finance the entire car when you do not consume the entire car? Why does the car dealership want to be repaid the entire $30,000 by the end of the fourth year, when the car may still have 50% of its value? It is because you are financing a purchase and not financing the asset.

If you were to your own bank, you could establish your own rules and require a repayment of only the value of the car you used during the given time frame. Since the true cost of the car is really only $26,000, not $30,000, and assuming the car will still have $11,000 of value four years later, shouldn't you be paying back only $15,000? Paying yourself back $15,000 over four years, even at an 8% rate, your car payment to yourself would be only $363. That is 42% less per month than what the car dealership is going to collect if you take the 0% loan. Can you think of any use you might have for $262 per month you do not have to pay? The $262 per month invested or saved at 5% for a 35-year-old until retirement 30 years later is almost $219,000 toward your retirement nest egg, if you find a suitable tax-free investment.

If you utilize the two keys to secure financial freedom stated above, this becomes real, actual money in your pocket.

Lesson #2: What I was taught to be true about large purchase financing that has turned out not to be true, is that you do not have to make monthly payments for the entire purchase price, only the portion you actually use, as long as you use yourself as a bank.

In the car example, you have restored $15,000 of the car value you used, and you still have a used car worth $11,000. Trade in the used car, couple that with another loan from yourself for $15,000, and purchase another $30,000 car ($30,000 less $4,000 cash back).

If you keep the discipline of saving an otherwise unnecessary monthly payment (because the loan was paid off) when you purchase the next car, you will be saving another $262 per month for twenty-six years. If you earn 5%, that will be another $168,000 for your retirement, if you find another tax-free investment or savings vehicle.

Lesson #3: What I was taught to be true about large purchase financing that has turned out not to be true, is that all consumer debt is not bad debt, not when you are the bank and treat yourself like the bank!

12

Quick Lessons

The average American wakes up every morning to the abrupt ringing of an alarm. They get out of a bed that was financed, shower and puts on clothes that were purchased with a credit card. Then they hop in a car that they purchased with a "0% loan", uses gas purchased with a credit card, and goes out for lunch charged to the same credit card. We do this every day to work a job and contribute to a 401(k) plan which can deducted from income and result in a reduction of taxes otherwise due. Remember, anything due today that you do not pay today, is a loan. Then at 5:00 PM, they get back into that financed car, use up the gasoline that was financed only to return home to a house that is financed. Then, they try to pay it off those debts as fast as possible with the money that was earned at work. As they pay down the mortgage, they cut away at the very tax reduction they have been working all day to achieve in the 401(k). Sounds like heading down the road of life with one foot on the gas and one foot on the brake.

It is a vicious circle that we have all been taught early in our adult lives. It is no wonder the average American cannot get ahead.

I now realize that some of the things I was taught while preparing myself as a CPA, have turned out not to be true. There are a few other quick lessons that can be derived from common sense if we just stop and think about them.

Capital Is Critical

Most people do not have a money problem; they have a capital problem. They make enough money; they just have not capitalized, meaning they have not put enough money away to decide whether to use their own money or to use someone else's money. Remember, every purchase is also a financing purchase. You are either going to use someone else's money and pay them interest or use your own money and not receive interest. Recapturing or reclaiming the interest paid or not received is vital in achieving your financial potential. This is an important subject.

Average Americans do not understand how important capital is. They just go paycheck to paycheck and hope they do not spend more than they take in. However, our cash outlays are not as predictable or as level as our incomes are, thus putting us in the position of needing capital. The choice is either our own or someone else's. Successful businesses understand this principle, or they would not be successful and would be out of business. A business would never try to exist day to day, sale to sale. A business knows it must have a reserve or capital set aside, or an approved line of credit from the outside, to carry it through certain cycles of business. However, even some business owners do not transfer that knowledge over to their own personal lives. They live paycheck to paycheck, with no reserve or capital set aside. It is not that they do not have enough income; they just spend it all with little thought to tomorrow or the perils that await them.

It really boils down to whether we will be the customer of the bank all our lives or learn to be the bank. You must put yourself in a position to have the choice. Then learn to decide whether to use your money or use someone else's money.

Most of our hard-earned and saved money is in the two most inaccessible accounts: our 401(k) plans and our homes. We put as much money in our 401(k) plans and get our houses paid off as quickly as possible. Because we do not understand the rules, we are locked out of access to these stacks of money. When we look at our 401(k) plans, we hope someday they will come out of their growth slumbers and skyrocket just when we need it. But if the market soars, what will happen to interest rates? They may go up to compete for your savings dollar with the market, as will mortgage rates, effectively locking us out of accessing the cash stored in our houses.

You want to be in control of all your money, but you will not be in control until you understand how important capital is. We start life using other people's capital and never learn to establish our own. We are too quick to get into the cycle of borrowing and too busy paying other people the interest they are due. If you were offered the opportunity of a lifetime, but it cost $10,000, could you have access to that much money by the end of the day? Would you lose the opportunity to earn 50% on that money by the end of the month? Your answer to this question will shed light on how well you understand the lesson of capital. You may have the money, but if it is spread out in places you cannot get to, then it has lost its value as liquid capital.

Do not Get Discouraged

One of my favorite movies is Secretariat, the story of the winner of the Triple Crown of horse racing. I like this movie because it illustrates the importance of planning our estates wisely. If not for the miraculous career of this once-in-a-lifetime racehorse, the estate of an entire family would have been wiped out by the estate taxes that were due.

However, I was also struck by the incredible career of the horse Sham, perhaps the greatest runner-up ever to run a race. Sham came in second in the very races that made Secretariat famous, except the last, the Belmont Stakes.

It was at the Belmont Stakes that Sham had the greatest chance to beat Secretariat. It was the longest race of the three jewels of the Triple Crown of horse racing. Sham was thought to have more stamina as a distance runner than as a sprinter. Secretariat, on the other hand, was a sprinter, and his value as a distance runner was the question of the day. Leading up to the race, as the movie points out, the last piece of direction Secretariat's trainer gave to the jockey was, "Run him hard, just don't burst his heart." Sometimes that is how we look at our investments. We run them hard, hoping not to burst the account by not knowing when to stop and get out. We burst the bubble.

In the case of Secretariat, he showed that distance was not a problem, and he beat the field by an incredible thirty-one lengths! His heart proved strong, and the horse that came in second was not Sham. It is said that it was Sham's heart that broke during the Belmont Stakes, as the horse lost to Secretariat by forty-five lengths, finished last, and never raced again. We must be careful whom we compare ourselves to. There will always be the story of the person who sprinted throughout his entire investment career and never looked back—an investment career as spectacular as the career of the great Secretariat. But those are once in a lifetime. Do not be discouraged by spectacular stories. Consistently fight the fight and finish the race.

Sprint Racing vs. Marathon Running

I am also fascinated by the label, "the fastest man on earth." This title goes to the person who runs the 100-meter dash faster than anyone else. Currently that title belongs to Usain Bolt, whose fastest time in the 100 meters is 9.58 seconds. At the other end of the spectrum is the marathon—26.2 miles. If math were the answer to all of life's challenges, to win the marathon, all you would need to do is divide 26.2 miles by 100 meters and get this guy to run the marathon 100 meters at a time. Obviously, this will not work. Math is not the answer.

The sprinter is done after 100 meters; he cannot even go another 100 meters, much less 26 miles. A sprint is over quick. In a sprint you are always concerned with who is right behind you and wondering where you are now. People look at their money in the same way, always looking over their shoulder, wondering where they are now. A marathon is forward-looking, with an eye on the finish line 26 miles away. It does not really matter who is leading as the runners leave the starting line. Your money is marathon money, not sprint money. For a married couple both age 65, it is likely that one of the spouses will live to see the age of 92 or more. That is a marathon! It does not matter much where you are after 100 meters. It is not how you leave the gate; it is how you finish. Marathon runners just want to establish a steady rate of speed that they can maintain over a long period of time. It is not how you start; it is how you finish.

Cash Value in the First Year

Life insurance cash values in the first year look much like marathon running. Getting out of the gate is not as important as finishing the race. Most of the time, what is deposited as the first year's premium may not be seen as cash value until after the third year. Cash value reflects only what you can recover from the policy if you choose to terminate it prematurely. It is no reflection of its long-term value other than it represents how much of the death benefit can be collateralized if desired as a loan. Therefore, when choosing a permanent life insurance contract, in the first few years, never put money into the policy that you are going to need to access right away. That all begins to change later, when the cash value is at least equal to your annual premium. In the most efficient permanent life insurance contracts, your lack of liquidity is only evident for a couple of years.

Hypothetically, let us suppose you put in $20,000. Let us further suppose that at the end of the year, you get a statement that says you have a cash value of $7,000. It appears you have lost $13,000. Your perception is correct, and if you chose to terminate the contract, you would indeed lose $13,000. However, if you consider this a marathon run, the only thing you have actually lost is access to the $13,000, just as the only thing the marathon runner has lost is the prestige of being the early leader. Being the leader after the first mile is irrelevant; finishing first after the 26th mile is the objective. The only question you must ask yourself is this: can you do without the use of that money for a while?

It is an interesting question, because we rarely ask ourselves that question when we participate in our employer's 401(k) plan. In most situations, we lose access to all that money until we reach 59 ½ years of age, and then only if we have terminated our employment with that employer. You can always access that money earlier than 59 ½, but that comes with two penalties. The first penalty is 10% of the amount withdrawn before being adjusted for the income taxes due as an early distribution penalty and the second penalty is the loss of your job. That is a steep price to pay for liquidity. Yet employees line up at the office of the human resource manager to sign up for this every day.

Instead, pretend you can start the life insurance policy in year two or three and look at the cash values in year three or four of the policy. In those years, your cash values can be equal to and greater than the amount of money you put in as your premium each year. The access to your cash value in the first year is limited for various reasons, including keeping the contract within the guidelines of the IRS's definition of life insurance. This is extremely important because compliance with the guidelines insures the tax benefits of a life insurance contract. If the contract falls outside of the guidelines, the tax benefits provided to the cash value part of the contract are forfeited. The contract merely defers the taxes due on the growth of the contract, much like for an IRA. There is a big difference between deferring the taxes due to some uncertain date, at an uncertain rate, and deferring the use of the money a few years. Remember, you do not lose the money; you just defer the use of the money.

Reporting requirements are not the same for life insurance companies as they are for other financial institutions. What the life insurance company must show is only what is available. What would your 401(k) statement say if it had to disclose only what was available? If your 401(k) had a loan provision included in its design, it could show 50% of the account value. If there were no loan provision or hardship withdrawal provision, it would have to show $0 until you turned 59 1/2, and still footnote the statement indicating that you had to terminate your job first.

Remember that in your permanent life insurance contract, you are entitled to more than the cash values. Your heirs are entitled to death benefits if you should meet with an untimely and unanticipated early death. Another way of looking at the loss of liquidity in the first years is to consider the opportunity cost of this loss. Without the permanent policy you would have had to supplement your estate with an equal amount of death benefits through a term insurance policy. The cost of the term insurance is the opportunity cost of your lack of liquidity in the early years of the permanent policy. Let us consider that you are a 35-year-old husband and father of a young family. To permanently forgo access to $13,000 in the first year of the policy at 5% is $56,000 for 30 years to age 65. The cost for an equal amount of term insurance at 5% opportunity is $142,000. Which opportunity cost would you like to incur: $56,000 that you will have completely recaptured in your cash values at age 65, or $142,000 that the life insurance company, in a term insurance policy, will keep forever?

Remember that you are in a marathon run, not a sprint race.

Accumulation vs. Distribution vs. Generational Transfers

Financial strategies are completely different depending on whether you are on the accumulation side of life or the distribution side of life. The most dramatic financial tool for accumulation is likely the worst financial tool when it comes to distribution. That Jekyll and Hyde investment is often anything that includes market volatility and the postponement of taxes. That does not mean that you should avoid the qualified plan; a 401(k), 403(b), SEP, or IRA, or anything in which you receive a deduction from taxable income when you make your deposits. However, these financial tools should be used in such a way as to have options when you take distributions for retirement. The overuse of a qualified plan may result in retiring in a higher tax bracket than the tax bracket that was used to calculate the tax savings when the contribution was made. Getting the money out in the lowest tax bracket is the key.

Furthermore, when estates transfer from one generation to another, another set of rules is set into motion. As the baby boomer generation ages, they are leaving behind a bountiful amount of money to the next generation. Distributions at death are different under certain circumstances. Prepare now. Know how qualified plans, mutual funds, and life insurance, just to name a few, are treated, and structure their ownership and inheritance rights, now. How you allocate between your investments is especially important. As an example, qualified plan money left to a charity from your estate is not taxable to the charity. However, qualified plan money from your estate is taxable to your children at their tax rates if they inherit this money. Too often, the charity receives the income tax free life insurance death benefits, and the next generation receives the taxable qualified plan. It should be the other way around. Give your children the tax-free life insurance and the charity the qualified plan asset, which is tax exempt to them by virtue of their charitable organization status. Both assets are tax free to the charity, only the life insurance is tax free to our children.

In retirement and at death, it is more about your strategy rather than the financial product. You may have been product focused throughout your accumulation life; now it is all about strategy to access it. The sooner you move to managing your money strategically, rather than purchasing that "hot" product, the more efficient your distribution years will be.

Avoid being overly concerned about the rate of return **on** your money. Instead, be concerned about the rate of return **of** your money. I have never seen a grocery store allow you to pay by showing them the rate of return on your money. They require cold hard cash.

A Golf Analogy

When you start to shift your thinking from focusing on the best financial product to following the best financial strategy, you begin to understand that several products are necessary to play the game. In the game of golf, you are allowed to play with 14 clubs. The one that gets the most attention and is practiced with the most at the range is the one that hits the ball the farthest: the driver. The driver is always the most updated club in the bag, as we try to find the newest and best driver to hit the ball farther. Hit it hard and hit it far. However, hitting it hard and far is fraught with risk. Fairway rough, water, sand, and out-of-bounds stakes are just waiting for your ball. You do not always end up in the fairway, but it does go far. It feels good when you swing the driver exactly right. The driver is great, but the best club in the bag is the putter. You use the putter on every hole; the driver is left in the bag on several holes and is usually taken out of the bag only 14 times if that often.

The pros know that you swing the driver for show, and you putt for dough. Master the putter, and you will cash more championship checks. In your finances, the driver is your accumulation tool, but if you want to get the most money out of your assets, you need to master the putter. Permanent life insurance is the putter because it enhances many accumulation products. It can also save an errant financial start, just as a putter can save par after an errant drive. Obviously, it is not the only product in the bag. You need all the others. But you cannot get through a game without a putter. Unfortunately, many of us try.

Accuracy is more important than distance on the green. The putter is the peak performer.

Get Your Social Security in a Lump Sum

What? And tax-free? Oh, come on, now!

Most people become extremely disappointed when they finally retire and realize that because of the way they saved for retirement, they are going to have to pay taxes on their social security income. For the average successful couple in retirement that could amount to over $250,000 or more.

By the time retirement rolls around, most people have their homes paid off. The good news is that you no longer have a house payment, but the bad news, as shown in previous chapters, is that all the equity in the house is earning 0% and is completely unusable. The retirement plan is to make the house the children's inheritance and live off social security and the 401(k). Excessive distributions from a 401(k) require you to pay income taxes on your social security. "Excessive" is defined by the IRS as $32,000 for a married couple and $25,000 for a single individual or marriage survivor (2021 definitions of excessive is no different than the first edition of this book 10 years ago).

Excessive? How do you avoid this unfortunate surprise? Let us say your social security income is $1,500 per month and you own a home worth $300,000 without a mortgage debt. If you were able to obtain a conventional 30-year mortgage, with 20% down, your mortgage payment would be $1,140 at 4%. What does this achieve? If you use your taxable social security payment of $1,500 each month to pay your tax-deductible mortgage payment of $1,140, you will end up with an excess $360 each month and a lump sum of $240,000 tax-free. To be completely clear, the $240,000 comes from the loan proceeds of the mortgage and is a tax-free distribution; the taxes on the social security income are offset by the interest paid on the mortgage if you qualify to itemize your deductions.

The best application of this strategy is someone who does not really need social security to live on. And instead of waiting until that someone dies to give the kids the value of the home, he or she can give an early inheritance while still living. Why wait till death to give your heirs the value of your home?

This is just one example of utilizing a retirement distribution strategy rather than an investment product. This example also illustrates the power of not leaving your wealth in your home. The survivors of natural disasters know this lesson well.

Disaster Lessons

A natural disaster comes most unexpectedly, even if we live in disaster-prone areas. Whether you are victimized by a broad-brush natural disaster such as a hurricane, flood, forest fire, or earthquake, or you live through a more local disaster such as a tornado or personal fire, if your money is stored in your paid-off house, your physical disaster may just be beginning. As you read, do not misunderstand; I believe that your house should be paid off, but the value of your home should be in a safe side account, and you should still be carrying a mortgage.

Under any of the above disasters, assume your paid-off house is demolished. The flood or earthquake coverage maximum may be significantly less than the value of the house, or you may have a financially significant deductible. If all your money is being stored in your house, where is the money that you need to rebuild? A $250,000 limit will rebuild only half of the $500,000 house.

What if there was a mortgage? The insurance maximum is still only half of what it will cost to rebuild, but the bank is now on a major hook as well as you. The bank has major legal resources behind the insurance loss. The bank may not be able to work it out, but do you really want to have to wait for the bank and the insurance company to sort it all out? In a broad-based disaster, you are not the only claim. Money in a safe side account that could have been used to pay off the mortgage would be available to begin the rebuilding process in a safe environment until the insurance mess is all sorted out.

What if it is your business that is destroyed? The COVID-19 virus did just that for many small businesses. Now more than just your life has been disrupted. But, with the money in a safe side account and not in the bricks and mortar, you can be back in business. You do not have to wait on the insurance company or government, as in the case with the COVID-19 virus. Employees are re-employed. Customers remain loyal. Money tied up is not very usable. Money available is king.

If you are forced to rebuild, access to capital is a very comforting feeling. Unfortunately, too many of us must live through it to understand it. This last statement is attributed to the mayor of Port Arthur, Texas, whose home survived Hurricane Rita only to be destroyed in the aftermath by fire. In his interview, he did not say, "Boy, I'm sure glad we just paid off our house." Instead, he said, "The worst part is that we just paid off the house last month." If his home were a safe place to store his cash, why would that be the worst part?

One Last Example of Having a Strategy of Coordinating Financial Products

If you are interested in tax-deferred growth, it is available in more than qualified plans. What do you like best about your 401(k) plan? If you are like some, you will say, "I'm saving all of those taxes." Now you know that is an untrue statement. You are not saving taxes, just deferring them to the future at a time in which you do not know at what rate your savings will be taxed. If you like tax-deferred growth, how are you enjoying your 401(k) today as you are building it up? Do you have fond conversations about it with your spouse and family? What do the kids think about your 401(k)? They do not know anything about it? Kids say the darndest things. They may say, "What? You are putting all that money in your 401(k), but you cannot use it for 30 years? You will be old then; will you be able to enjoy it?"

Why not put the money somewhere where you can enjoy it and still have it grow? How about on the beach or in the mountains? Like to ski, fish, enjoy the outdoors? Wouldn't it be nice to put that 30-years-from-now money somewhere where you can enjoy it today?

A second home in the mountains, or a condo on the beach, gives you similar tax-deferral opportunities to those of your 401(k) plan. Your 401(k) deposits are tax-deferred, and your second home's mortgage interest is tax-deductible if you itemize your deductions. From a tax deduction perspective, there is no difference. You are not paying current taxes on the income used for either the retirement plan deferral or the interest paid. The 401(k) is supposed to increase in value, does it? The real estate property is supposed to increase in value, can it? Perhaps it can, more so than before, ever since the meltdown of the real estate values in 2008, and the Covid-19 virus economic recovery.

In what other ways does a vacation condo compare to a 401(k)?

1. At retirement, both will need to be liquidated to finance your retirement. The sales proceeds of the 401(k) are taxed as ordinary income. The sales proceeds of the condo are taxed at more favorable capital gains rates.
2. At death, both will pass on to the next generation. The 401(k) will be taxed as ordinary income. The condo will be income

tax-free upon its sale since investments receive a step up in basis for the heirs at the owner's death.

3. You are limited to how much you put into your 401(k) plan. You can deduct the interest on a loan up to $750,000. The combined limit for both your principal residence and your condo.

4. With your 401(k), you get annual statements. With your condo, you get annual pictures of your family vacation to review.

5. Your 401(k) gives you no enjoyment during your working career. Your condo gives you a lifetime of memories.

6. You are locked out of your 401(k) until you are 59 ½. With your condo you get two sets of front door keys.

7. If you use your 401(k) early, you are penalized. If you use your condo early, not only can you receive immeasurable opportunities for your family, but you can also share them with your friends and your children's friends.

8. With your 401(k), even if you do not need it, you must begin liquidating it at age 72. With your condo, if you do not need it, you can always give it away to another family member.

When you are planning your finances, think outside of the box. Just make sure to weigh all the advantages and disadvantages of your options. There is not just one magic product, but with your imagination and creativity, anything is possible.

13

What I Believe

I believe ...

1. The financial decision-making process is more important than any product available.
2. Everyone ought to be out of debt. The probability of financial success is greatly enhanced if you are debt-free.
3. There is a minimum amount one ought to be saving.
4. People ought to know where they are today. How are you doing financially?
5. People are entitled to know if they will be financially successful if they keep doing what they are doing.
6. People are transferring their money away unnecessarily. People ought to know where this is happening.
7. Cash values are more valuable than home equity.
8. Your mortgage should be paid off as quickly as possible.
9. Your mortgage is paid off when you have the money to pay it off, not when you terminate the mortgage contract.
10. Taxable income from assets that are in a taxable environment for a long period of time has a devastating effect on your ability to consume your money.

11. Opportunity cost is a real thing. If you lose a dollar, you not only lose the dollar but also what that dollar could have earned over time.

12. Qualified plans defer the tax and the tax calculation to some uncertain time, at some uncertain rate.

13. The #1 concern of people approaching retirement is running out of money.

14. People approaching retirement want to talk to someone about the issues confronting them.

15. Over the next 25 years, distribution strategies will be more important than accumulation strategies for most Americans.

Afterthoughts

One of the most difficult things to do, is to describe somewhere you have visited and words are inadequate to describe it. Sometimes, when I meet with clients and try to explain these concepts, words just are not sufficient. However, it is more than satisfying, when clients have embraced the concepts and have experienced the results, so much so, that they refer their friends with enthusiasm.

It is very much like having visited one of our great national parks, whether that is Yellowstone, Grand Teton, Mount Rushmore, the Grand Canyon, Yosemite, the Appalachian Trail, the Great Smoky Mountains, the Pacific National Monument, or Pearl Harbor, the experience is the same. Your words or even, the pictures you take, just do not do it justice. The best way to explain the experience, is to take the members of your audience with you the next time you go. Watch their facial expressions and body language as they experience what you have been trying to tell them.

If you embrace and apply the principles contained in this book, you will have the same experience I have had. I wish I could be there to see your face!

15

The One Truth I Was Taught
That Will Always Be True

I am writing this updated edition of Confessions of a CPA during the COVID-19 Pandemic. This great virus and the interruption to life it has caused, will be a defining moment in the history of the United States and the World. There are only a few events in history that have changed the future. This will be one of them. It will share a place in our history books as does Good Friday, Pearl Harbor and the 9/11 Terrorist Attacks. These events changed our lives. This one will too – we will never be the same.

The choice is ours whether we will be better for the Pandemic or worse. How we respond will determine our future destiny.

It reminds me of the Saturday between Good Friday and Easter Sunday. That Saturday in between was either a dark day or a day full of anticipation. It depended upon how those in 33AD looked at the events of that Friday. It was the day Jesus was hung on a cross and suffered a torturous death. Some saw it as the end of a rebellion against the Roman Empire. Some saw Jesus, as their promised King and Conqueror. His death ended the potential earthly reign of their promised, Messiah. Others understood that his death would usher in a new eternal kingdom. One that would defeat death itself and solve the problem of personal sin. However, these followers had to wait for the promised Resurrection of Jesus Himself on Sunday morning.

This is the truth I was taught that will always be true: Jesus in human form is God, he lived His earthly life, He suffered and died as payment for my sins, and He rose victorious from the dead, defeating death itself, and He ascended to Heaven.

Scripture tells us that this we can know. The apostle John concluded his first letter to the Christian Church like this, "These things I have written to you who believe in the name of the Son of God, so that you may know that you have eternal life." He did not write 'think', 'hope' or 'wonder'; he used the word 'know'.

Saturday can be confusing. But it is not, when we know what is coming. Scripture also says that no matter what, we must "reach forward to what lies ahead".

Whether it is eternal life or COVID-19, how we look at this 'Saturday' will make all the difference in the world.

About Bryan S. Bloom, CPA

Bryan began his financial career immediately following earning his CPA credentials and Bachelor's Degree in Accountancy from the University of Illinois. Later he earned his Master's Degree in Business Administration from the University of Illinois Executive MBA program.

His career started as a staff accountant for the State Universities Retirement System of Illinois where he eventually became the Chief Financial Officer. After 19 years of experience in public retirement matters, he worked for 5 years with Benefit Planning Consultants, Inc. BPC, Inc. is a third-party administration CPA firm overseeing private retirement plans. He is currently associated with The America Group and has been assisting individuals in their personal retirement planning for the last 21 years.

Bryan earned Million Dollar Round Table membership within his first four months. He earned the VIP of the Year award from Ohio National Financial Services that same year. In 2010, Bryan was recognized by Ohio National with their Chairman's Navigator Award, highlighting him for the personal integrity he exhibits with his clients and business relationships. In 2020, Bryan was recognized with the Norman J. Tschantz Lifetime Achievement Award to honor his many achievements as a financial services professional.

Bryan and his spouse of 40 years, Pam, live in Champaign, Illinois, and are avid fans of the University of Illinois Fighting Illini.

They have two daughters, Callie, and Corrie, two fine sons-in-law, David, and Kyle and four wonderful grandchildren, Emmie, Ellie, Coen and Everlie.

You can contact Bryan at   bryan@bryanbloomcpa.com

About Bryan S. Bloom, CPA

Bryan began his financial career immediately following earning his CPA credentials and Bachelor's Degree in Accountancy from the University of Illinois. Later he earned his Master's Degree in Business Administration from the University of Illinois Executive MBA program.

His career started as a staff accountant for the State Universities Retirement System of Illinois where he eventually became the Chief Financial Officer. After 19 years of experience in public retirement matters, he worked for 5 years with Benefit Planning Consultants, Inc. BPC, Inc. is a third-party administration CPA firm overseeing private retirement plans. He is currently associated with The America Group and has been assisting individuals in their personal retirement planning for the last 21 years.

Bryan earned Million Dollar Round Table membership within his first four months. He earned the VIP of the Year award from Ohio National Financial Services that same year. In 2010, Bryan was recognized by Ohio National with their Chairman's Navigator Award, highlighting him for the personal integrity he exhibits with his clients and business relationships. In 2020, Bryan was recognized with the Norman J. Tschantz Lifetime Achievement Award to honor his many achievements as a financial services professional.

Bryan and his spouse of 40 years, Pam, live in Champaign, Illinois, and are avid fans of the University of Illinois Fighting Illini.

They have two daughters, Callie, and Corrie, two fine sons-in-law, David, and Kyle and four wonderful grandchildren, Emmie, Ellie, Coen and Everlie.

You can contact Bryan at   bryan@bryanbloomcpa.com   ████

"Discovery is seeing what everybody else has seen
and thinking what nobody else has thought."
Dr. Albert Szent-Györgyi,
Nobel Prize Winner

What were your discoveries? Write them here and share this
book with others.

CPSIA information can be obtained
at www.ICGtesting.com
Printed in the USA
BVHW092239240822
645456BV00006B/11